GOD QUESTIONS

Meeting the Living God

WILLIAM J. O'MALLEY, SJ

Paulist Press
New York / Mahwah, NJ

The Scripture quotations contained herein are from the New Revised Standard Version: Catholic Edition, Copyright © 1989 and 1993, by the Division of Christian Education of the National Council of the Churches of Christ in the United States of America. Used by permission. All rights reserved.

Cover image by Hefr/Shutterstock.com
Cover design by Christina Cancel
Book design by Lynn Else

Library of Congress Cataloging-in-Publication Data:

O'Malley, William J.
    God questions : meeting the living God / William J. O'Malley, S.J.
        pages cm
    ISBN 978-0-8091-4936-0 (pbk. : alk. paper) — ISBN 978-1-58768-527-9 (ebook)
    1. God. I. Title.
    BL205.O45 2015
    231—dc23

                                                                2014045198

ISBN 978-0-8091-4936-0 (paperback)
ISBN 978-1-58768-527-9 (e-book)

Published by Paulist Press
997 Macarthur Boulevard
Mahwah, New Jersey 07430

www.paulistpress.com

Printed and bound in the
United States of America

For Fran Henderson

CONTENTS

INTRODUCTION: WHY BOTHER?

—"I treat God the way I treat my parents' *other* friends."

—"We don't talk about those kinds of things at home."

—"Guilt trips are bad for you. They screw up your life."

—"It's unfair of you to tell us we should be grateful to whoever invited us to be here. I think it's selfish of God and our parents if they want gratitude."

—"If she wants sex as much as you do, who's gettin' hurt?"

—"I've got plenty of time before I have to think about that kind of stuff."

—"I didn't ask to be born."

—"Look, I cheated because my dad'll kill me if I fail."

—"My parents? They're the *last* people I'd tell!"

—"Religion's okay in school—for a while—and for little kids and very old people."

These are actual quotes from students, and I've been teaching for half a century! A different approach to the God Questions draws out the hidden resistances that have been there all along. There are many more powerful influences on what kids value than religion.

Because these quotes express where my audience is really coming from, my approach has been forthright, down-to-earth, and relentlessly *honest*. Some students have called it "in-your-face," and I'm happy and rather proud to agree. The people I teach have always been almost ready for college or already there. I have no time to pussyfoot around these important questions. First, I think they're among the most crucial questions

1

anyone can face. They're the bedrock on which all other value questions ultimately rest. Most important, this is possibly the *first* time your students and children will be asked to confront them not as children but as emergent, reasoning adults, and also quite likely the *last* time. Right now is surely the last time they can do it with your help.

I hope you'll allow me to be as, if not more, forthright in these pages.

Through the years of my teaching young students, we've come through many transitions: the late '60s with "Don't trust anybody over thirty-five," and the befuddling aftermath of Vatican II with the brainless years of bells and banjos, collages and "Kumbaya"; the deluge of priests and nuns rejoining the laity, followed by a cold war between Catholic conservatives and liberals, with one side wanting old-time catechism conformity and the other working for genuine personal acceptance and conversion; the lackluster attempts to make the liturgy closer to the Latin rather than to the human heart; and then the profoundly disheartening molestation scandals.

My life has been devoted to converting baptized young Catholics who've never once considered personally *choosing* to be Catholic. I confess that it would be far, far easier for me to convert an animist Aborigine clapping two boomerangs in the Australian Outback than to make a genuine Christian out of one of your children—even the best of today's first-world kids: the decent, smiling, ultimately cooperative, *nice* kids. Who needs God when you have a credit card and a cell phone?

The odds are stacked against me. Before I get them in late high school or early college, they've been brainwashed continually to infantile greed by the electronic babysitter. If you're as aware as most parents are of germs, surely you must have noticed how the media has been infecting their minds and values. They've seen people engaged in what is clearly foreplay, but not a single pairing has been married. (You never noticed that?) Not just in films and TV, but in video games that are now accessible on a phone, your children have witnessed more gore and death than Napoleonic veterans and have vaporized countless humanoids without the slightest compunction.

Economy, which used to mean "thrift," now stands for a prodigal way of life that encourages the gullible to spend as if credit card bills never come due. The Economy has taken the place of an overall matrix of meaning that long ago was Christendom but without any intrusions from airy considerations like God, human dignity (morality), or virtue. It has its scriptures (*WSJ*, *Forbes*, and the Dow-Jones); its priests (investment bankers, the Fed, and brokers); its saints (Jobs, Trump, and Zuckerberg); its rituals (the Super Bowl, World Series, and the Olympics), and its heavens that justify any sacrifice or demand (Las Vegas, Broadway, Hollywood, and the 'burbs). It's not uncommon to hear businessmen who worship weekly talk about "those 'wetbacks' feeding their too-many kids outta my refrigerator," without the slightest whisper of contrary ideas from someone as socialist as Jesus.

For longer than they will sit in front of all their paid teachers put together, your kids have *already* spent more time in front of the TV teacher, who makes the important—love, sex, and death—trivial, and the trivial—abdominals, hair, and complexions—important. It has taught them morality by engrossing examples, in color, three to four hours each day. Every week, since they sat up in diapers in front of the electronic babysitter, professionals more skilled than most other teachers have instructed them in what makes humans happy, successful, fulfilled—and it has nothing whatsoever to do with any god other than the Economy, nor, as any fool could tell you, with Christianity. Forget Catholicism! How does an hour at a desultory Mass stack up in appeal and radical persuasion about basic values next to that daily fare? Contrasted even to a crummy garage band concert, church propaganda is pretty limp, useless, and to be perfectly honest, counterproductive!

A local New York City TV station began the late news, "Ten p.m. Do you know where your children are?" Parents could ask where their children's minds are—*really* are. Will being Christian or Catholic have even the *slightest* influence on their choices of college, career, spouse, or their own children's upbringing? Will it intrude in any significant way on their regard for themselves; their self-esteem? Will their motives, when faced with a chance to cheat, to engage in casual sexual encounters, or to reach out to the unattractive be any more altruistic than the children of atheist and agnostic parents? Nifty questions, which demand informed parental answers!

Just as a check, at least to assess whether you might be deceiving yourself about the depth of your family's or your classes' Christianity, here is a condensed version of the Sermon on the Mount—what many feel distills all Jesus' hopes for humans. It's what Christians claim to be their personal basic philosophy of life, the norm for all their choices. Ponder and ask yourself how much of it your children would wholeheartedly accept, how much they'd gag at, and how much they'd simply hear and shrug their shoulders at anyone whose ideas were so "out of it" and naïve.

Lucky are the poor...the mourners...the humble...the integrity-hungry...the merciful...the pure of heart...the peace-makers...the persecuted...the insulted and falsely accused....*You* are the salt of the earth....Let your light *shine!* If you're angry...insulting...you'll be liable to hellfire....Harbor no grudges. Beware lusting with the eyes. Let your word be yes or no; nothing more....Turn the other cheek....Give to anyone who begs from you....Love your enemies....—and on and on.

In all honesty, before you consider accompanying your youngster, or other peoples' youngsters, through these pages, do you really *buy* that gospel yourself or do you just "go to church"?

When I arrived at my first school appointment after seminary in 1965 ready to teach English, the principal suddenly asked me to take over two religion classes. No problem, I thought! However, I found that the class text was childish, pandering, and deadly dull. More important, "These kids don't even believe in *God!*" That's when I first wrote *Meeting the Living God*, which, unlike the new official bishops' *Syllabus*, does not start from the top down, from revealed truths to dutiful acceptance, and which hardly has a chance with its intended audience. Instead, it starts at the only place any genuine learning can start: curiosity and puzzlement. This approach starts from where young people *are*: in defensiveness brought on by catechetical overkill and from the cynical world in which they grew up—where successors of

Abraham Lincoln are forced to resign or be impeached for lying and for engaging in oral sex in the Oval Office; a world where tabloids have reporting teams 24/7 on the prowl for actors, athletes, and clergy degrading themselves and others, and where half of all students check "Agree" to the statements "In business, anyone simply has to curtail moral principles" and "Children of parents who have worked hard *deserve* more of this world's goods than children of parents who haven't."

Over the years, the changes have become dramatic. If Booth Tarkington wrote *Seventeen* (1916) today, he'd have to retitle it *Twelve*, and if Holden Caulfield were a teenager today, he'd have died of an overdose, and *Catcher in the Rye* (1951) would be a short story. I'm convinced that the students I teach have little or no sense of the transcendent; the "other-worldly." Recently, I asked a college class, "Can any of you tell me something you and your peers consider 'sacred, holy, and inviolable'?" There was a long silence. Then one young woman said, "Babies, maybe?"

My inquiry also convinces me that "sin" is now lost in the unlamented past. Unlike what was once an embarrassingly puritan and sin-sensitive Catholicism has yielded to a catechesis where even longtime Catholic students come to me convinced that "guilt trips are bad for you." For years, I've had students write things like "I feel bad enough when I did the wrong thing. Why should I keep thinking about it?" and "Thinking about what you've done wrong only gets you down. It's healthier to forget about it." No one seems to have suggested to them that without guilt what you get is extermination camps, ten million African AIDS orphans, drive-by shooters, infant corpses in dumpsters, and date rape—all in "civilized" societies.

Consistently, I've asked both students and science teachers, "When you teach sex education, do you just teach the mechanics?" Of course! "You mean that you say nothing of the light-year difference when two *human* beings are engaged in it; the psychological investment, and the critical dangers to the persons?" They reply that science is science, just as "church is church, and business is business." It reminds one of the defenses at the trials of Nazis at Nuremburg: "I was only following orders" or "Such questions are above my pay grade."

Like any other unaffiliated science teachers in "values-free" schools, Catholic physics teachers explain—patiently and with admirable clarity—that inert matter suddenly began to grow, and that vegetative matter then evolved into animated, mobile, sensitive matter, which in turn evolved into humans. From my experience, every single one of those teachers skillfully avoids confronting the inner prickly questions, like "How?" and "Why?" None of them seems to have faced the challenge of how molecules suddenly "*learned* how to make crude copies of themselves," as Carl Sagan so cavalierly asserted. Those grade school, high school, and college science teachers simply assume it was inevitable that animals would sooner or later get around to harnessing fire, the multiplication table, and quantum physics, just like that! I'll bet you did, too, and still do.

Finally, is there anyone who can claim that the liturgy does much to ignite the souls of those whose parents never urged them to become acquainted with their souls or postpuberty God?

Ultimately, is it justified for parents to leave the "God Questions" to others?

Do you remember your *own* reaction to religious education at the age when you suddenly began to smell rats everywhere, fearing nothing more than being hoaxed and looking unsophisticated? Was it tedious, irrelevant, repetitive, and unengaging? (Am I getting warm?)

In offering to become involved with your child in confronting the God Questions, this might be the very first, and possibly the last, time he or she ever faces them as an *adult*. Previous attempts at interesting them in God have been in terms that (might) satisfy children as yet incapable of nuanced thought but are now doing trigonometry and macroeconomics. Even if they go to a Catholic or Christian college and are required to take two theology courses, at least some colleges are satisfied with "Spiritual Massage" and "Scandals of the Renaissance Papacy."

Just as the introduction to *Meeting the Living God* is "Why Bother?" it is necessary to ask adults that same question here. Is it worth your time, effort, and commitment?

GENERAL SUGGESTIONS

The most important preparation you can bring to this task is the resolution to be *honest*: "I simply can't figure out what that text means" or "This approach is so radically different from the way I was taught." As you read the text, make a note or put a question mark next to places like that. Your candor will make this a genuinely *shared* quest, not a top-down "instruction." Confessing your lack of perfection honestly will enhance your credibility rather than diminish it, because honesty requires more confidence than pretense.

Just as *we* are no longer docile children, neither are the young people with whom we're probing ideas. Furthermore, too many parents feel that their child is "still my baby" even when the baby has produced more kids. They act as if adulthood doesn't *really* start even with a college diploma and a first job. Conversely, too many youngsters like to believe that adulthood and all its privileges—not its demands—clicked on at the emergence of physical puberty. Contrary to those misreadings of the facts, it is hoped that both older and younger can become more "fluid." The elder is willing to rethink; the younger ought to be learning how to think. They are not static states but processes requiring effort.

You're talking to an emergent adult, like a butterfly partway out of the cocoon—fragile and wary, no matter what the façade may indicate. However, one fact to focus on is that this emergent adult is a person whom "everybody"—including, at least tacitly, you—believes is capable of dealing with calculus, *Macbeth*, as well as driving a hugely expensive vehicle without a parent, and even being alone in it at night with someone; choosing a college for which you'll lay out hundreds of thousands of dollars, and quite likely attending beer parties unsupervised by adults. Off with the training wheels! Neither church dogmas nor parental certitudes are any longer acceptable or effective. Your audience, no matter how pliable, comes from a country whose demand is "*Prove* it!"

For the adult parent and teacher, this is also a whole new "position"—a new attitude. Not only is the conversation a light-year from baby talk, it is also a long way from adult-to-child. However, it's not yet quite adult-to-adult. Even though adolescents mouth clichés like "Experience is the best teacher," they don't mean your experience; they mean *theirs*. (To which a facile response is "You mean you'd actually have to experience rape or castration to accept that it's undesirable?" With more than a half-century in the classroom, I've learned the utility of *reductio ad absurdum*.)

First, the fact that you're talking to one another across the narrowing divide in this new way is at least as important as the content. It's beyond sports or fashion talk, or texting on your phone, and way beyond the god-awful "How was school?" This is an engagement not only of differently formed minds, but of differently influenced souls, values, and sensitivities. At the same time, some adolescent tribulations have varied only on the surface from the same adolescent trials in the caves. Why would anyone think homework is any more appealing to them today than it was for us? If religion was held at arm's length when we were teenagers, why would it be intriguing for them now? Always remember that genuine learning begins with *curiosity*, or it's just wasted time.

Any student who claims to be *lazy* is misusing words. Put them at a concert or a championship game and they're anything but lazy. The correct word is *unmotivated*. As Nietzsche said, "Whoever has a *why* to live for can put up with almost any *how*." You put up with a lot of tedium and frustration at your job if you have a felt *purpose*. The trouble is that, just as teachers never told *us* why we should endure math or history or Shakespeare or religion, they don't do it now either. Just like oxen at the plow, you do it because you're told to; because everybody has to do it; because we've always done it; or because it gives access to food. The types of responses these days are "But my parents don't read novels"; "My mother's a lawyer, but she hires someone good at math to do her taxes"; "My dad has a secretary to do his proof-reading"; and "I'll endure it, but I'll put as little into it as I can get away with."

Thus, the overall result of schooling is developing habits of docile cooperation, not to acquire anything useful—except the diploma, which you need even to manage a Wendy's.

Instead of stories about having to walk to school five miles, through hip-deep snow, uphill (both directions), can you at least ponder the possibility of being honest about your own adolescent anxieties? Can you talk fearlessly about your own bewilderment about sex or embarrassing infatuations? Maybe the acid test is whether you can talk about how utterly lonely masturbation is?

When you come to a topic your adolescent finds troubling or indigestible, don't say, "This is what that means." Instead, try asking, "First, what does it look like from where you are? Help me understand what it seems to mean to *you*."

The questions that this text raises are truly, objectively important. As the text will keep insisting, God's existence is a matter of incontrovertible *fact*. If God exists, no amount of disbelief will make God disappear. If God truly does not exist, the fiercest belief or its near universality or its consistency in human history will not *make* God real. Is there any entity outside our minds that justifies belief? Such a question deserves respect only if this Creator is a Person who freely chose to allow me to exist—Someone to whom the very gift ought to make any honest recipient profoundly grateful.

The alternative is that there is no need for gratitude, but as a result we exist only temporarily, after which we will cease to be real, as will everything we attempted to achieve. Even our children will cease. Yet we're cursed, as only humans are, with a yearning to have some sense of purpose, some *reason* to keep going when life becomes unrelievedly unrewarding. However, in a godless reality there is *no* purpose—except the temporary purposes we impose on our lives before annihilation—and hell begins the day we were born.

At least at the outset, forget Catholicism and getting them to Mass. For a while, forget even Christianity. The only question is "Are we created with a purpose or are we merely accidents?" Don't try to get them to Mass just to "save their souls from hell." If they worship, let it be because they need to show thanks (*Eucharist* is "to give thanks") for the chance to be alive and a personal appreciation for the unmarketable value of integrity.

Finally, this shared quest will be meaningful to both parent and youngster only if the question of your child's belief or disbelief in God is more important than whether he or she chooses to be a Democrat or a Republican.

I
_____

HOW CAN WE BE SURE OF ANYTHING?

1

WHAT VALIDATES OPINIONS?

Everyone is entitled to his own opinion, but not his own facts.

—Daniel Patrick Moynihan

This foundational chapter is the scaffolding on which every opinion—no matter *what*—hinges, pivots, hangs, lives, or dies, whether it be the morality of Hiroshima, backseat sex, the consumption of Coca-Cola or Lysol, views on cancer, stomach gas, the coach of the Mets, the validity of your signed check, the testimony and jury deliberations at a murder trial, deciding a career, choosing a spouse, buying a house, or accepting God.

This chapter is crucial if a group of intelligent individuals decides that "the situation" justifies a war that will destroy the lives, bodies, and minds of a generation on each side. It will also prove useful at every dinner table argument.

WHERE'S YOUR *EVIDENCE*?

Failure to engender the avoidable but undeniable requirement of evidence has been an issue in all but a very few young people I've *ever* taught.

—My opinion's as good as anybody else's.
—You're *blind*, ump!
—Everybody on welfare cheats.

> —Society just decides what's right and wrong and then
> teaches us what to do.
> —Homosexuals *choose* to be that way.
> —Guilt trips are bad for you.
> —Oh, Mom! *Everybody* does it!
> —Faith is a blind leap in the dark.
> —Morality changes from age to age and from culture to
> culture.
> —It depends on the *individual*!

Many people call those unconsidered bumper-sticker slogans "thinking for yourself." They're pulled off the rack at a thrift shop, picked up with the peanuts at the local pub, or snagged in the powder or locker rooms.

Opinions are self-justifying: "That's *my* opinion, so *back off!*"

It is my suggestion that many people—even some with degrees—don't truly know how to think. Of course, they can "have ideas," but any child can do that. They can parrot back the last and loudest opinion they've ingested: "I saw this program on *Nova.*"..."Haven't you read Christopher Hitchens?"..."My chemistry teacher said"..."Everybody knows...."

Opinions are everywhere, but you wouldn't go broke giving a buck to everyone who'd researched an idea or even read a single book about it.

In all these years, the hardest obstacle to crack is *confident ignorance*. The trouble is, first, that it's huge, heavy, and dug in deep. Second, it's blocking the first tunnel under the battlements of vested self-interests. Whether you are a teacher or a parent, you must first face this obstacle or rap your knuckles raw on the Rock of Gibraltar.

Everybody has a right to voice an opinion. However, we have no right to have our opinions automatically *respected*—and there's the rub! Feel absolutely free and welcome to express your opinion, but in all fairness, you're risking an outburst of laughter from your listeners. *They* have *that* right, as well. Prudence would suggest that you don't voice an opinion—at least not vigorously—unless you have solid evidence and persuasive arguments for it.

You'll also never go broke betting on dumb. P. T. Barnum and others have made millions on that valid supposition. "Dumb" has nothing to do with IQ or SATs or advanced degrees. It stems from a lack of perspective—restricting "value" and "importance" to elements of fierce personal concern to oneself (vested interests), but—objectively—to anyone else would seem trivial. Consider two women, sincerely weeping: one over her child's coffin, the other over a rip in her Dior dress; or your parents' snappish responses compared to hints from your boss that you might no longer be needed.

In the movie *Twelve Angry Men*, consider what motivated their (every single person except the Henry Fonda character) initial guilty vote? Was it the objective evidence? What's missing from the ten vacuous opinions listed at the start of this chapter? Does their motivation make you reconsider any attitudes?

If "society" decrees what's right and wrong, was it then evil to hide Jews in Nazi Germany and slaves in the antebellum South? "But they *thought* it was right!" Okay, but if we both buy that "principle," don't complain if somebody who firmly believes this world's goods are unjustly parceled out takes your sneakers or your bike. One college student told me, "No one has a right to criticize anyone else's lifestyle." *Lifestyle* is the newest name for "morality," that is, doing whatever feels right at the moment. I responded, "If that's true, then World War II was one massively unjustified intrusion on Adolf Hitler's freely chosen lifestyle."

The Price of Teaching the Young

"And you will be hated by all because of my name. But the one who endures to the end will be saved." (Mark 13:13)

Taking a young person's unexamined "principles" and certitudes to the absurd is always effective, even though they'll rarely admit that. However, when their faces seem to be saying, "Right now I *hate* you," rejoice, not just because Jesus loves you for forcing the truth on the kids you love, but because you've gotten *inside* their defenses! They don't like it because you're making sense—which no catechism has ever done before. They're beginning to see not only that some attitudes are wrong, but *why* they are wrong. They're beginning to interiorize the truth, accept it, and yield their freedom to it—as they must with gravity and deadlines and alcohol.

Help them to learn that they must *gather* evidence, *sift out* the important, and arrange it in some logical relationships (an *outline*), which enables a *conclusion* and the chance to ask for a *critique*. You will have invited them beyond the schooling that teaches the skills of literacy and computation and dutiful ingestion of facts into *learning*—the humans-only quest to *understand*.

If they can truly learn the importance and skills of gathering evidence and honest reasoning, there will be no need for the Ten Commandments or the *Catechism of the Catholic Church* or the Codes of Civil or Canon Law! Laws are made for folks too dumb or too self-centered, too narrow, and too haphazard to figure things out for themselves. There should be no need for thinking people to have laws against savaging their own children or driving drunk or abrogating others' property or violating anyone's body (including one's own). However, societies, in fact, forge laws to save us from ourselves, but *forged* is not the same as "made up" or "fabricated out of thin air." Wise legislators see that some actions inevitably turn out badly, and so, like prudent parents before their children have the power to think for themselves, establish no-no's. It's as simple as that; reasoned laws are not arbitrary.

"But I want to be *free*—like the people on those reality bachelor shows or like the people in *People* magazine and on the late-night shows, and like actors and athletes who are always forgiven. They don't have to be cautious all the time. It's like having a cop for a Siamese twin. Everybody says guilt trips are bad for you, and they *are*! I *hate* that!"

You're absolutely right! Guilt can become evil on its own. Some sad people let themselves be devoured by it. However, guilt is necessary! What would it be like if nobody felt restricted by guilt? (Did he or she read *Lord of the Flies*?) What would happen if all the cops in the city went on strike and refused to budge? What would happen if the students in your year were stranded on a deserted island with plenty of roots and fruits but no adults? Who would take charge? What kind of qualities would that person need? Who'd start the first fight? Who'd be the first one killed? (Why do I assume somebody would be killed?)

It's also essential to point out the difference between guilt and shame. Guilt honestly accepts that "I did something bad." Shame says, almost always unjustifiably, "I'm a bad person."

No matter what heat and fury is generated on both sides of the abortion question, neither side is composed of inflexible, pot-boiling fools. However, neither is the issue as cut-and-dried as unthinking people on either side *feel* (versus reason). The less you know—the more facts on the other side you refuse to admit—the more certain and impassioned you become.

"The tree comes to me, tells me that it's there, what it is, and how I can legitimately treat it." What decides the morality of abortion? The fetus!

On one side, it is *not* merely a part of the mother's body. The *fact* is that half the fetus's DNA is completely different from that of the mother. Any forensic doctor can verify that, and can also verify that the tissue from this "entity" is certifiably human and not chimpanzee. It is close, but not the same. If you leave it alone, it will establish that undeniably. However, it is also undeniably true that nearly half of fertilized ova fail to implant in the uterus, which would argue that if an undeniable human *person* exists from conception, nearly half of humanity died before being born. That is at least imaginable, like 99 percent of all creatures since the Big Bang no longer existing. However, such imagining leaves the benevolent and purposeful God with even more explaining to do.

However, I have found the analogy to the hunter being unsure of whether what's rustling the bushes is human *really* hard for even the most resolutely convinced pro-choice student. How can you kill a fetus—no matter what the hellish cost of not doing it—when you're simply not at all sure, and not sure in the sense that we require for other justified homicides: "beyond any reasonable doubt"?

FOR REFLECTION

First try to answer these questions yourself before asking your teenager to respond with the same honesty.

1. Try to describe what God meant to you when you were a fifth grader.
2. How has your image of God and your relationship with God changed since then?
3. If the relationship has deepened since then—or deteriorated since then—can you give the reasons for that?

2

THANATOS: THE DEATH WISH

Denial ain't just a river in Egypt.

—*Mark Twain*

Invariably, when I've asked parents what their primary tasks are, the most predictable responses are, first, to shield their children from harm, and second, to give them the best they can. (There is no need to ask what comprises "the best." It almost always has a dollar sign.)

There's a deep but unrecognized problem here. If parents pull that off *too* successfully, they actually hamstring their children—sometimes worse than abusive or absent parents—by protecting them completely from suffering. Many college students have never had to make their own money, even for entertainment. Many have never been to a wake or a hospital. Many are shielded from inconvenience or from an "F" grade even when they fail to rise to a rightful challenge. Any teacher who gives a "D" to a student's essay that is bilge *is* the enemy. Such shielding damages students for life as badly as delaying weaning till they're five, because it shields them from the inexorable truth that life is simply not fair and deprives them of the opportunities to become self-sufficient adults.

One father put this ironic impoverishment perfectly, "When I was in high school, I made up my mind that my kids would never have to wade through all the crap I did. And I *did* it! I gave them everything other kids had back then that made me jealous—except what I *got* from wading through all that crap: spine."

Beyond that, parents provide a superabundance of toys, electronics, sports equipment, and chauffeured rides between enjoyments, all of which have a habit of warping their children's perceptions of reality. They can become so truly spoiled that they take that for granted—which is a poor lesson for coping with real life, marriage, mortgage, and parenthood. Even worse, they can become so used to being pampered that they never learn gratitude, which many young people see as an unfair crimp on freedom.

Children are ill-served if we give them all the skills to play volleyball only to send them out to make a living in a minefield.

No one, I suspect, yearns for the "good old days" when kids rode bikes or walked to the one-room school with holes in their soles, then came home to chop wood, muck out barns, eat the same supper as last night, and huddle with a precious book around an oil lamp. However, it didn't seem to cripple the future for Abe Lincoln, Mark Twain, Thomas Edison, Dale Carnegie, Henry Ford, or Colonel Sanders. For them, disadvantages were an advantage.

Today, the majority of buyers for enraged rap "music" are white, middle-class males. Teenage suicides from ghetto hopelessness would be painfully understandable, but not country club hopelessness. *Unless* they've been led to believe that life can deliver what life simply *cannot* deliver: perfect fathers; unfailing doctors; brilliant lawyers; sterling cops; and problems solved as quickly and satisfyingly as courtroom shows and math "prompts." (For some reason we're no longer allowed to say "questions" or "tests," but "assessments"; nor even "failure" but instead, "underperformance" or "delayed success.")

Our children's lives are completely full of distractions. Some may recall that Victorians used the word *distracted* about the mentally ill. Such distractions present countless ways that their minds get skewed from the truth and from accepting life on life's non-negotiable terms. Here, this chapter suggests that parents, for the kindest motives, might incautiously connive in that avoidance.

NOT A STAGE BUT A PROCESS

Just like weaning and potty training, adolescence is an *invitation* to grow up. The suffix, *-escence,* indicates the word is inchoative, that is, a process begun but not yet complete, as in "convalescence" or "obsolescence." Unlike less-developed and more humane societies, we get the idea that adolescence is a kind of "state of suspension," like *Star Wars* cosmonauts in womblike pods. It's a withdrawal of all unpleasantness, the way the father of the Buddha shielded him obsessively as a boy from the Four Distressing Sights: poverty, sickness, old age, and death.

On the contrary, adolescence isn't a stage but a *process,* exactly like the one you patiently supervised turning an infant into a child. Every day coaxing, "Okay, come on! Just a *few* more steps! C'mon!" Coaches do it, too: "We'll take three more laps today....Stop doggin' it!" Coaches know their job is to toughen kids up, if they want to get in the Game. Adolescence is the same. Week after week, you (ought to) push them to grow more and more adult by rising to more difficult challenges. Becoming a physical grown-up happens automatically; becoming a mature adult takes time, patience, and, maybe more than any other parental price, being disliked—even hated for a while. All good teachers have to learn to accept that high cost of loving.

By all means, *tell* them what you're doing! Tell them that you're doing what Glinda the Good Witch made Dorothy do; what Gandalf and Obi-Wan Kenobi and Dumbledore did: providing conflicts without which a story isn't worth listening to; offering them the sandpaper against which to hone their adulthood.

Check out any of the growing-up myths from the *Odyssey* and *Beowulf* to *The Wizard of Oz* and *The Lord of the Rings.* Notice that in every one of those time-tested tales, the hero or heroine is often an orphan living with aunts and uncles—Dorothy, Luke Skywalker, Harry Potter—or forced to cope with a wicked (read: demanding) stepmother, who's replaced the kindly Fairy Godmother. In the 80,000 years since we crept out of the caves, this century seems to be the first time in the course of human history that future providers, spouses, and parents are being prepared for those tasks by being deprived of being deprived.

21

One bright young woman who came back from a long stint within the Jesuit Volunteer Corps put it close to perfectly, "It took me six months just to unlearn privilege."

Freud saw what every other student of the human soul has seen over this long trek. He observed that every individual or group was motivated at the core by one of two fundamental drives: Eros, the Life Wish, which craves challenge, and Thanatos, the Death Wish, which craves simply to be unbothered. Darwin saw it too: "Evolve, or die!" Maybe your religious education teachers never told you, but that's also the innermost *core* of Christianity: death can bring resurrection. *Meeting the Living God* says:

> That's why "senioritis" is evil. The death wish.
>
> The children of Thanatos are Self-Absorption and Inertia, and their children (the grandchildren of the death wish) are many. Among them, Prejudice, Herd Need, Protective Indifference, False Humility, and— the pride of the litter—Fear of the Cost. They are all enemies of freedom, because the cost of freedom is thinking for oneself. But, for most people, thinking for oneself just takes too much effort. Witness all those kids anesthetized in the "study" hall. (39)

The one grandchild the book doesn't confront directly is the Lethargy engendered from being so consistently spoiled and addicted to distractions: fear of silence and solitude, horror of any limits on what *ought* to be an uninterrupted spring break between puberty and marriage. Something gets lost about the middle of first grade: *curiosity*, when learning becomes the serious business of the SATs, which now supposedly sit like the Roman Fates, determining future lives.

Be warned. Remember your own religion classes, when well-meaning teachers winged around really heavy (but to us utterly weightless) words like *soul, love, grace,* as if we had the slightest clue what those words entailed. It was probably because the teachers themselves had never personally dissected them. Learn before you teach!

ANOTHER NEW WRINKLE
(IN TEACHING)

You've got to accentuate the positive
Eliminate the negative
And latch on to the affirmative
Don't mess with Mister In-Between.
                    —Lyrics by Johnny Mercer

After more than fifty years as a priest, I can't think of a single problem brought to me that wasn't rooted in a lack of self-respect, whether it be unwanted pregnancy, temptations to suicide, bright kids failing or dogging it, or cheating. If students had been led by those who guided them out of childhood to apprehend and value the sacredness of their souls—their selves—they would never degrade that self by cheating on a quiz that next day they'll forget or go for the cheap lay or undersell their talents and their gratitude to their parents. Instead, we establish hawk-eyed proctors, which only encourage their inventive cunning.

What if we dared to move *beyond* the negative, animal, childish fear of punishment to the positive, human, adult motivation of being a self to be proud of—of interiorizing an appreciation of decency and integrity rather than a guileful avoidance of punishment?

Every young person, in fact, every human being, has an inalienable right to respect; more respect than we'd give any other animal or a vegetable or a rock. That demand is based simply on the way we're *made*: more inwardly gifted than rocks or rutabagas or orangutans. The Declaration of Independence says that human rights are God-given, inalienable, self-evident, but in recent years, countless parents—out of the best of short-sighted motives—insist that their adolescent children should get *more* than respect. They also need *praise*, so they can be saved from negative feelings about themselves. They should *not* be *upset*, despite the fact that, since before Socrates, the whole *purpose* of adolescence is to *be* upset and to rise to new dignity by surmounting those challenges. After all, that is what *Hansel and Gretel, Cinderella, Jack and the Beanstalk, The Wizard of Oz, Star Wars,* and *Harry Potter* are all about!

The conviction that children should never be upset and the insistance that everybody get a present—even at someone else's birthday party—is debilitating, as is the idea that everyone in a race must get a medal, which renders the race meaningless. Similarly, there is the decision that no senior should be kept off-stage at graduation, even with two full-year failures—"assessments" and "delayed success." There are many who spend their lives helping kids become adults and who are furious about such gratuitous conferral of worth on the unworthy.

Nevertheless, like all one-sided, stupid beliefs, there's an important truth at the core of such idiotic exaggeration. Every young person's *humanity* does demand respect from others—just as the feelings in a dog and the food value in apples demand attention and befitting treatment. However, beyond human decency, an *individual* deserves approbation—rewards, praise, accolades—*only* by rising to challenges, and a good teacher, which all parents are, finds ways to engender the conviction that the key to human happiness is not in achieving but in the *striving*. Life isn't a sprint; it's a marathon. You "win" simply by not quitting. If someone is to give a 100 percent, how could anyone but a sadist ask for more?

Respect, you deserve; *meaningful* praise you have to *work* for!

That panicky flight from upsetting adolescents surged into religion education, too. Nobody in charge told us the difference between *guilt* (I did a bad thing) and *shame* (I'm a bad person). So we pitched them both. When we fled from imposing guilt, we fled too far and balked at opposing even *legitimate* guilt. Guilt for a genuinely less-than-human act is like hunger in the belly, a strong healthy sign that something is out of kilter and needs realignment, like squealing brakes or an overbite. Guilt is good *as long as* the individual turns it into responsibility; the touchstone of adulthood. Until a youngster resolves to become a decent human being—a person of integrity—forget Christianity, which hasn't a chance without that firm basis.

Back in the dark ages when I was a boy, all education was a dualistic struggle in which everyone who was not a winner was a failure and the silver medalist was just the first of the losers; saint or sinner. The Economic metaphor ran roughshod over Christianity: God the Watchdog Money Lender. Probably then the most lethal and crippling command was "Now don't you go getting *vain!*" Thus, even honest pride in a job well done was a cause for shame.

In the wake of Vatican II, people with more sensitivity than genuine perspective turned the Lion of Judah into the Lamb of God, who *cherished* without *challenging*. Young people were told, even by well-meaning religion teachers, that "guilt trips are bad for you." Jesus is a "Warm Fuzzy" who forgives everything, even when you choose not to take responsibility for it. In countering that ill-advised correction, this book adopts an approach that is neither *Crime and Punishment* nor *Anything Goes!*; neither "Ya better watch out!" nor "Let 'er rip!" The motivation is not sin or hell, but "Do you want to feel honestly good about yourself? How can you have legitimate self-esteem—a soul you hold sacred—if you readily degrade that self?"

Try it! It *does* work because they *are* good kids; just maximally confused!

FALLIBILITY AS A PASSPORT

For as long as I can remember, the official Church scuttled about trying to whitewash or paper over the remotest whisper or suspicion of a hint that it had flaws, which, like the exam proctors who wore dark glasses and sat atop the desk, simply begged for fault finding. More recently, with people who found the Church no longer engaging, the purported reason was "all those rules." They were unaware that almost all of those rules were duplicated in the value systems of every society that ever existed. They were simply written for people too dumb or selfish to figure out for themselves that, if we owe existence to some deity, he deserves our gratitude, and if we're going to live together, we have to respect one another's inborn rights.

However, another obstacle—at least for me—was that those who were trying to sell Catholicism kept claiming *certitude*, which, despite my loyalty, I couldn't muster. Even before I was clever enough to see the contradiction, "something inside" sensed the incompatibility of certitude and faith. Moreover, having witnessed flaws in absolutely everything involving humans, I harbored a "heretical" suspicion that there were weaknesses within the Church and the *Catechism*, too.

Most recently were the priests' molestation scandals and, equally unnerving, the evident attempts by Church officials to cover them up. Like Ezekiel's mighty statue, all it took was one well-aimed rock to tumble the idol. For too long, the Church had assumed the impeccability of God, and because most people's faith in God was being sustained by faith in the Church, when the Church wobbled, God became less trustworthy, less engaging, and less worth even a weekly hour.

The old Ivory soap commercial was humbler, or at least more cautious than the holy Roman Catholic Church. It claimed to be no better than "Ninety-Nine and Forty-Four One Hundredths Percent Pure." Thus, the conviction that *appearing* to be 100 percent pure elicited trust was actually counterproductive.

The same holds for all teachers. This past quarter, one of the self-styled atheist college students in my class said at the end of the course, "I really listened to you because you were so honest." I made no pretense about Catholic doctrines with which I felt uncomfortable. I refused to deny them, but every student could intuit my hesitations. (No one could put me on trial for what they *guessed* I believe!) However, what intrigued my listeners was not my "unbeliefs," but the fact that I *remain* a Catholic. For me, being a Catholic Christian is more important than all its flaws packed together. Why? As Jesus said, "Come and see."

For example, I used to invite the students to tell me about the TV character Archie Bunker, and we'd list on the board all the distasteful qualities of a bigot. While Archie's no longer available, no matter when you deal with it, there's bound to be some publicized narrow-minded oracle, who burns Qur'ans in his yard or, conversely, explodes himself on a bus in the name of Allah. Once you've drawn out the basics of bigotry—"closed-minded opinions based only on hearsay, complete lack of experience or research, unbending, arrogant, and no perspective"—I say, "We'd all like to believe that we're not prejudiced, open-minded, live-and-let-live, yes? Well, how about unathletic boys, or overweight girls, or kids savaged by acne? How about homosexuals? Are you open-minded about them? Are *you* possibly a Little League bigot?" It makes them uneasy.

Then, I entrust my own weakness to the students. When I was a senior, my mom informed me that I was taking (call her) Catherine Cronin to her senior ball. Now, I'd gone to grade school with Catherine, and that was simply unacceptable. She was agonizingly shy, with frizzy red hair, granny glasses, built like six o'clock, and not a spark of personality. However, my mom was in a finishing school class with Medea, Lady Macbeth, Catherine the Great, and Bonnie Parker. So it goes without saying that I did, in fact, escort Catherine to her prom.

It was awful. I had no night-driving license, so my dad had to drive us. Gasp! So, we got there on *time*. We were the only ones! I tried every conceivable conversational ploy from the band to the causes of World War I. In response, I got nothing but "Hm." Then my pals started to show with their dates, elbowing one another and jerking their heads toward me, I assumed. It got worse. I was a heckuva dancer. Not so Catherine. Every second became a century, until finally, at 11:30, I said, "Well, it's getting late...." So I called my dad and we took her home.

Then I give the students the kicker: "What a selfish SOB I was." After all their fellow-feeling hooting over my teenage angst came dead, shocked silence.

I was telling the painful, honest truth. It was almost surely her first-ever date. Certainly, it was her first formal dress, but never once, not for a nanosecond, did I think of *her*. It was all about me: Billy the Pious Altar Boy, Exemplary Catholic, and Boy Scout. Selfish Swine!

That really works! Unlike the perfect-model priest, I was a fellow sinner. I knew what it was like to be ashamed, and not proud of myself. However, how could I set things right? It was years later when I realized how small-hearted I'd been. I had no way of knowing where she was, so the best I could do was resolve that, for the rest of my life, I'd keep an eagle eye out for all the Catherine Cronins I met, and I would try to make them feel important. Since then, I've directed fifty musicals, and in every one I made sure there were five or six girls in the chorus who were drab, homely, and uninteresting.

Adolescents have always been "counter." The cause is not only natural, but healthy: their physical pubertal changes are calling on them to develop a new attitude and posture toward the world and all those in it. One of the most harrowing aspects of the process is transforming from someone provided *for* into a *provider*. In the "natural course of things," they have to begin taking control of their own decisions and values, and as a painful corollary of that, they resent anything intrusive on their newfound ability to reason and on the freedom that thinking invites them to. They resist rules, schedules, and contrary opinions—especially those presented as infallible, unsubstantiated, and unarguable. Therefore, the universal *Catechism* and the new *Syllabus* are like offering teenagers more acne. I apologize, but it's unarguable!

If you hope to make adolescents value altruism, the sacred, integrity—much less a crucified hero condemned by both Church and state—be prepared for the long haul, and for a reassessing and reinforcing of your own taken-for-granted convictions.

Some parents believe that giving their children a sense of "the perfect parent," a bulwark they can trust—like the superb Atticus Finch in *To Kill a Mockingbird*—will guard kids from unnecessary anxieties. There's much to be said for that—for a while. However, sooner or later, unless you have access to perfection that no one but Jesus' Mother had, the disguise will slip. Little Toto will bark and grab the curtain, and the Wizard will be exposed. When Dorothy says that he's a very bad man, he gives her one more gift welcoming her to adulthood: "Oh, no, my dear. I'm a very good man. I'm just a very bad wizard." Any human is.

This is not sure-fire advice, but do you have the confidence in yourself and in your child's assurance of your loving that you could say, "Son, I was confused as hell about masturbation, too," or "Honey, when I was your age, I had this god-awful humiliating crush, and I saw the guy in Walgreen's today. I just stood there howling with laughter at myself"?

If adolescents have always built up resistance against intrusion, and if for centuries we've made the same mistake of trying to guide them with fear of the cost of misbehavior, one way that's rarely been tried to undermine those fortifications is to be vulnerable. Instead of, "This is what you'll do," how about at least trying, "Could you help me understand how *you* see this situation?" Just keep silent and really listen, with *their* ears and then ask, "What do you think would be a good way to help you feel better about the mistake?"

Why should your own bitter experiences be wasted?

A final piece of advice! In my experience, most young people's problems in this area aren't really with God, but with organized religion: all the rules, going to a lackluster liturgy, and the intra-Church bickering. Call a cease-fire on all those and don't clutter the board with too many different games at once. "Let's stick with just the three God Questions. Okay? If there's no God out there, we can save ourselves all those hassles and have time for another *Bachelorette* show."

FOR REFLECTION

I once invited a successful neurosurgeon who was also head of admissions for the University of Rochester Medical School to talk to a group of seniors. Since every college grad would need probably a 4.0 cumulative average even to apply to such a prestigious institution, I asked what would be his very first interview question to a candidate for his medical school. Without hesitation he said, "What was the last novel you read?"

Why do you think he believed that question was so crucial? (That's a question you simply can't answer from-the-top-of-the-head, without the effort of thinking.)

3

PRIMARY TRUTH: THE NATURES OF THINGS

An error does not become truth by reason of multiplied propagation, nor does truth become error because nobody sees it.

—*Mohandas Gandhi*

All this chatter about epistemology and twisted values seems light-years from the alleged topic of God. However, this approach to the God Questions is dictated by the belief that the receptivities of our specific audience have been skewed by so many good, bad, and inadequate information systems that the God Questions haven't a fair chance even of consideration, much less acceptance, if we fail to unskew the inner filters.

The most obstinate obstacle to any unpleasant truth is the conviction in the mind of the listener that opinions are self-justifying. "I have a right to my own opinion." This is true, but not a right that it be *respected*—not unless it's backed by solid evidence and honest reasoning. If everybody's opinion is worthwhile, there's no such thing as truth.

A first contributor to the buildup of that particular resistance is no one's "fault." It's very difficult to get cooperation—much less agreement—from young people *before* they're psychologically capable of grasping the reasons validating any assertion. How does one get young people to behave acceptably when they have no more grasp of *why* than an overactive puppy? They ask why objects fall, why I can bite the breadstick but not the cat's tail, and why I have to go to Mass. However, they're still without the wherewithal to see and appreciate the reasons. Consequently, the much too easy-to-hand responses are "Because I *said* so. It's the law. You have to have high SATs or live on the streets. Everybody has to take math. Go to Mass or go to hell."

Much of the "fault" is that parents and teachers have never reasoned why themselves. What validates many imperatives? In the minds of most kids, not only are "all those rules" as arbitrary as which side of the road you drive on, but they've come to believe (who knows how) that over the course of thirty thousand years the rules have *changed* radically. As one college junior said, "It used to be you had sex just with your husband. Then it was just with someone you really loved. Now it's more for recreation." What used to be called "rules of morality"—being a human being, more accountable than any other species—are now called, more flexibly, "lifestyle." To all intents and purposes, behaviors and attitudes are chosen nearly as randomly as tie lengths or bathing suits.

Who can tell whence springs that silliness? If guidelines for being a decent human being change, if what was moral and ethical twenty-five years ago no longer has any practical value, then we could burn down all the libraries—*reductio ad absurdum*—or at least waste no more taxes on them, since libraries have in great part existed so that some of us won't keep making the *same* catastrophic mistakes. The vested interest, of course, is instantly clear: nothing parents or teachers say has genuine pertinence in *today's* world and shouldn't intrude on my freedom to do what feels good. I doubt that any single child "reasons it out" that way, but the result is manifest.

The same will be true when we finally get to the God Questions: God would be the *absolute* limit on my freedom to do what feels "good"—the ultimate wicked stepmother.

Again, I would point to the unwitting and inculpable shortcomings of most early science teachers and books. All of them illustrate the evolution of humans using pictures, which little kids are never told were not drawn looking at live models. They move left to right in gradual and clearly segmented progression from a gorilla, to a hominid, to a sort of human, to a full-fledged naked modern man. The science teachers never get around to telling their class that those are *educated guesses*. We have the unarguable (segmented) bones and, knowing what we do about the flesh such bones usually support, we *assume*—with a lot of peripheral evidence and reasoning—what the muscle mass "must" have been. However, just as we can get to midlife with a grade school notion of God, we can go lifelong assuming that those pictures are *accurate*, when they're no more "accurate" than the tiny solar system picture of the atom or the old-man-on-a-throne God. Consequently, students are never cured—even in university—of the conviction that science is precise, certain, and reliable, while all the humanities are mostly hot air.

Those physical (surface) changes in humans are a rather trustworthy high probability. So are conclusions by experts about the psychological changes that "must" have happened to get from an ape to the sophisticated humans we have today. It's not *just* "automatic and biological." This is a crucial element science leaves out of its considerations. As humans became psychologically more elaborated and aware, they *must* have had to deal with problems, both within themselves and from living together. Those problems we handily summarize as the Seven Deadly Sins: pride, greed, lust, anger, gluttony, envy, and sloth. Either the society (parents, teachers, and elders) find ways to control these problems, or the community won't last long, especially the weaker members (cf. *Lord of the Flies*). We have libraries because we're not *just* animals.

At least for the past three thousand years that those libraries have kept accounts, human beings have been dealing with the *same* constant conflicts regardless of what *Survivor* and *Playboy* might suggest.

Another more recent abomination has been the almost universal confusion of "information" with "understanding." As I was walking to class the other day, I met another professor and said, "Ah! They're sitting there, like little birdies in the nest, waiting for the mama bird to bring them a worm." Following the same silly line, he said, "Well, I hope the worm is knowledge." To tell the truth, I gagged! What good is *knowledge*? If that's all you want, there's Google. What I'm trying to do is incite them to go *beyond* knowledge to some kind of *understanding*.

In class on another day, I was broaching the subject that has bedeviled every philosopher from Buddha to Karl Marx: finding some way to understand suffering. One young man, brow furrowed, began to tap-tap on his phone. Like a sunbather aware of the thinnest cloud of inattention, I asked what he was doing. He said, "I'm looking for the answer on Google."

He was *serious*! I love access to Google, but I'm going to find only *information* there. Like the *Catechism*, Google has no satisfying answers for the truly meaningful questions. Neither do dictionaries! Under "love," mine has thirty-three tight lines defining that important reality, and when I got to the end, I said, "I wish I knew as little about what love costs as that Noah Webster." Try researching these on Google and Webster:

— To what extent are experiments on live animals justified by the later application of those experiments to alleviate human torment?
— Did the American Civil War establish as fact the inhumanity of slavery?
— Are humans merely "rational animals," former apes with shrewder minds?
— Will heavy doses of vitamin C lessen the common cold?
— Is human sex simply the same activity shared by all healthy animals?

First, come and look. Study the objective facts. What does the object or action tell you about itself? How can you legitimately use it without violating its inner nature, programming, and value? Not just rocks, carrots, bunnies, and people, but dealing with repulsive people, envying more gifted others, demanding feelings of lust, frustration, food, money—the lot! Draw conclusions from the way each is made and about how to use it appropriately. If you're honest, I'll bet you come to exactly the same conclusions that men and women have come to for centuries: rape is evil; so is tormenting a cat, wasting food, and stoning children who look funny.

At this point, I bring into class a "mystery" bag containing four objects that are going to establish my credibility for the entire year. Like a magician, I pull them each out with a flourish: A rock. It tells me that it has mass, weight, some kind of electric "signal," and that it's inert. Then, *voilà!* An apple. It tells me that it has all the values of the rock—mass, weight, atomic signals—*but* that it can also take in food, grow, and reproduce, which no rock can "hope" to do. *They* tell me that I can safely bite the one, but not the other. Then a stuffed bear—all the qualities of the rock and apple, *but* it can move around, feel pain, sense danger, which the other two simply can't. The facts! Now, if I have eyes and a brain, I need no authority to tell me the differences. Then a human doll: all the aforementioned qualities *but*, as far as we can tell, it is the only one who can feel hope, regret, compassion for those we dislike, and guilt—as opposed to shame.

Humans are the only "objects" we encounter who can screw up—act less than our specific nature invites us to. You can prove that from the morning paper. So, can we put to rest all those ridiculous ideas we misread from science classes about humans being merely a minor shift from chimpanzees? Teachers told us that the DNA of chimps is only a whisper's difference from that of humans. They neglected to say that no chimp ever seemed capable of writing *War and Peace* or the Declaration of Independence—a major omission! It wasn't intentional, but it was lethal.

FOR REFLECTION

Probably no question is more real to an adolescent than "Who am I?" After puberty, all the evidence seems to have been tossed into a cocked hat. Consider what concrete, specific evidence you have to prove that you are, indeed, a good person. Such a question has always been intended, at the very least, to lessen apprehension about a young person's sense of personal worth. Since I presume that the number of helpless serial killers taking this course is small, I know these kids have far more good in them than bad. However, they've heard far too often: "Don't you go getting *vain!*" I base this conclusion on the thousands of reflections that declare discomfort in writing down evidence of their own goodness.

Another consistent disappointment is that they all seem to have a genetic antagonism to *concrete specifics*. "Oh, I try to do good things....I really love my family...." How does it *show*? What kind of *evidence* would a court expect in order to convict you of goodness? The whole purpose of the question is to give them an unarguable case that they are *worth* treating with *respect*. That goal should outweigh the two goals most parents have: to shield them from harm and give them "the best." That "best" ought to be a self that they will never treat cheaply.

Right here, a parent could say, "Okay, let me start you off with the 'testimony' part of your answer. This is what I testify on your behalf as being a *terrific* person."

4

WHOM DO WE SEEK?

The only way to get somewhere, you know, is to figure
out where you're going before you go there.
                                        —*John Updike*

This chapter is an hors d'oeuvre—a brief sidebar in the midst of a seemingly inappropriate detour into repairing the damage to our listeners' ability to perceive the truth without undue influence. It's a reminder that this book seeks to explore the God Questions.

Too many people—parents, teachers, and those who control religion syllabi—operate under the false assumption that young Catholics all firmly believe in God. The understanding of theology assumed by theologians who generated the *Catechism* and *Syllabus* is the time-tested definition *fides quarens intellectum*, "faith seeking deeper understanding."

In my experience, I've rarely found a youngster who has anything near what the most generous would judge to be authentic, grounded faith. Nor have I found many who were honestly as interested in a more profound understanding of God as they are in a diploma and a well-paying job.

Furthermore, those in control of the matter and manner of religious instruction believe that, since the creative, purpose-giving God *is* so objectively important, young people fittingly accept that as true and govern themselves accordingly. They value God in an honest human being's life. This is like claiming—as Canon Law *does* (97, #2)—that the power to reason clicks on at age seven—an assertion roundly scorned by anyone who's begotten or taught a high school sophomore. It's like asserting that all young people are, by nature, grateful for their parents' sacrifices. The same people discuss marriage as if it occurs primarily in the bedroom.

My experience suggests that most of the young people I've taught—no matter what their claims—seem no more influenced in their basic attitudes and values than any of the theoretical atheists or agnostics or indifferent thinkers I've encountered. Their responses to role-play moral dilemmas on cheating, business ethics, casual sex, and career choices seem to confirm this view. Furthermore, the ones who do strongly profess a belief in God seem, at least to me, to accept God for a lot of wrong reasons: "My parents tell me; the Bible tells us; the Church tells me, and most people have believed in some 'Higher Power.'" In fifty years, no student has ever said, "I've done solid research, checked a lot of the firm arguments for atheism, and made the decision for God." I can't recall any student saying or writing, "I still have the real person-to-Person friendship with God my parents introduced to me as a child."

Among young people who do profess a belief in God, the "god" they describe or profess a belief in often either falls far short of what most experts would agree approximates the God who seems to demand attention and gratitude, or is an understanding so acceptably wishy-washy, undemanding, and permissive that God becomes completely ignorable.

Anyone who disbelieves my strong assertions about the readiness of today's young for the message of Christianity really should read *Soul Searching: The Religious and Spiritual Lives of American Teenagers* by Christian Smith and Melina Denton. It contains interviews conducted with teenagers for the National Study of Youth and Religion. The book is encyclopedic and exhaustive (and the graphs can be skipped by the nonexpert), but the study shows that the majority of today's young people do *not* have "religion" in ways similar to what most people believe religion to be: a person-to-Person connection with God. Rather, the researchers found that they hold a "moralistic therapeutic deism," that is, religion fosters subjective well-being and lubricates relationships. God loves us, but doesn't expect too much of us beyond not hurting people. God is to help people succeed in life, to make them feel good, and to help them get along with others. God is like the Fairy Godmother at the other end of a 911 number. The study claims that the greatest influence shaping teenagers' religious beliefs is their parents.

As a preliminary bout with the long-range questions, the only four positions available are Yes (theist), No (atheist), Maybe (agnostic), and Who cares? (indifferent). Some students have assured me that they come from homes where religion, that is, God, is very strong, but those voices have become few to none over the past twenty years. What's more, standing as it does in the midst of a welter of strongly, enticingly asserted pagan propaganda, the very strength of some parents' convictions is sometimes more repellent than attractive. (Surely not always.)

Parents attempting to travel along with their youngsters' explorations of these questions could try—with as much objectivity as one can muster, like a medical doctor—to see what the real content of "the God words" is in their child's present stance on the Mind-Behind-It-All.

Taking into account all the contrary influences on adolescents' values since they were infants, it's difficult to see how the question of a God, who set up the Game, with its rules and pitfalls, could be that pressing a question—not when ranked against physical attractiveness, sports, fashion, and the opinions of others, especially the cruelest and most popular. This does not intend in any way to belittle young people. When you cut them out of the herd, they're wonderful and free. However, we have to remember their lives are an endless hall of mirrors— report cards, clothes, complexions. Every commercial is an invitation to judge oneself, as are the eyes of every classmate of either sex.

Such a negative assessment is not claiming that their indifference to God is a culpable fault! Like the rich people Jesus presents trying to squeeze through the eye of a needle, modern kids have a great many toys and distractions. Many are like the rich young man he invited to come along, but who "walked away sad, for he had many possessions." The propagandists offer values much more meaningful now and in the long run, "when I get out in the *real* world."

Consequently, I'd judge confidently that for most, even the best, religious ideas and practices fade into indifference, not in a blameworthy way, any more than an adult's valid claim, "I really ought to exercise more." The reason for parents and teachers to bring these questions into more meaningful focus now is that this is most likely the first, and last, time they'll be pushed to consider these questions as adults.

Argumentative "atheists" are usually the smartest kids in the class. Again, in my experience, their negativity has less to do with reason and almost *never* with a personally experienced run-in with the God of Job who afflicts the innocent. Most of them have been too protected-subsidized-spoiled to be genuine gut-atheists. For most of them, a declaration of atheism is merely one more act of pseudo-adulthood, like spike heels or a bare midriff or a boy's earring or facial hair. Like those other fads, the atheism is so superficial, it can't last.

Agnosticism seems the safest claim, and it is by no means insincere. However, even though at the moment they seem so young, as Andrew Marvell wrote, "At my back I always hear Time's winged chariot hurrying near." Since we all know how long it takes for an idea to sink in and become interiorized as a genuine value "versus" grudging conformity, it's never too late or too early.

ATTITUDE

In the past, and for many still today, the preceptive method was always unquestionable. "This is the doctrine, ingest it, and conform." No one, except suicide bombers, is susceptible to that formula anymore. "Because I said so," simply won't work. Neither will "the Church" or "the Bible." The response is "Prove it." Of course, no one can prove it, not with enough unarguable evidence and reasoning to compel assent, no more than you can "prove" love without a whisper of doubt. All you can do is offer *evidence* and argue accessibly to a reasonable conclusion—not certain, but highly probable—even Moses, Jesus, and Aquinas couldn't do better than that!

However, that different approach does suggest—no, really *demands*—a different attitude. Physics and math teachers don't get any ornery objections to the validity of the Pythagorean Theorem or the value of Pi, but these God Questions are seeking a commitment. They're asking young people who have *just* arrived on the brink of independence to give up some freedom, in deference to a God they can't see and are taking only on your word. Just as they'll have an easier time with the SATs if you have read to them a lot as toddlers, they'll find God Questions easier if you have made them more personally connected to God at that same pre-logical time. Be that as it may, you take them where they *are*.

Consequently, except for the very few, religious education for young people is a matter of *salesmanship*—and it's a buyers' market. There are far more enticing products out there vying for their acceptance, and they're much more appealing than a corpse on a crucifix!

As any good salesperson takes for granted—and few teachers or parents do—if you want to sell a product, you have to *create a need* in people who haven't really felt the need till now. How do you sell shoe polish to someone who rarely wears anything but sneakers? How do you sell ice makers to Eskimos, or hockey skates to Bedouins? How do you get people you love to value light when they've never been lost in the dark, or to feel grateful when they've never felt genuine need for too long? How do you get a person to value the gift of life when you've never taken them to a wake?

INADEQUATE GODS

One of the most foolish arguments against God says, "Humanity fabricates a benevolent Divine Being because we haven't the guts to admit" as Matthew Arnold did do courageously:

Ah, love, let us be true
To one another! for the world, which seems
To lie before us like a land of dreams,

So various, so beautiful, so new,
Hath really neither joy, nor love, nor light,
Nor certitude, nor peace, nor help for pain;
And we are here as on a darkling plain
Swept with confused alarms of struggle and flight,
Where ignorant armies clash by night.*

It's all a hoax to keep us going and keep us in line. Albert Camus was unafraid to accept the inevitable that in a godless universe, the two greatest curses are intelligence and hope—the inner human yearning for answers and survival, when the fact is that there are no answers and no one survives. (Remember some time ago, in order to give your children joy, you lied to them about Santa Claus. Correct?)

The reason the made-up God is a ludicrous accusation is the fact that even the most *limited* human being could come up with a "better," more accommodating God than the one with which we have. In a radio talk in 1933, Alexander Woollcott repeated a much-attributed chestnut: "It seems as if anything I like is either illegal or immoral or fattening." Why did the God who gave us free will not allow us to use things any way we want to, without the bothersome consequences?

Here the point should be made: the tree comes to me. There are limits to what entity could "qualify" as the ultimate "Mind-Behind-It-All." I can't define an orange as something similar to a rock, or a chimpanzee as a human. The object in question doesn't live up to the demands of the definition. The same also applies to God. If there is *some* "Mind-Behind-It-All," he/she/they can fit the job description *only* if that primal entity is not just a mindless "It." Only a mind can give purpose, just as this pre–time/space Causal Person cannot be less than *we* are, dependent on us for anything.

The "God" we're trying to validate here is a personal Being who has freely chosen to allow us to be in this life and love these people. Otherwise, we have to accept the only alternative: that the mindless Force of evolution simply stumbled one blind step

---

*Matthew Arnold, "Dover Beach," c. 1851.

too far and came up with a species made to seek final answers when they don't exist.

"The tree" tells me that it exists, what it is, and how I can legitimately handle it, just by the way it's made. So, too, there are qualities that every human has discovered in his or her self. Such qualities don't seem, as far as we can tell, to intrigue/trouble/ engage any other animal we know: we are aware of an *order* everywhere we look—the universe, the "progress" of evolution, the gradual development of each human being, and the seasons. Most of us have also experienced "losing ourselves" in *play* and feeling an exhilaration of existing beyond the ordinary. Perhaps some are too young to have a serious need for *hope*—a reason to keep going when "everything" seems to cry, "Doom!" (That's why adolescents, at least, should not be kept from wakes.) Hope is a gritty clutch that defies reason. We also have an inner demand for *justice*—that people who've been screwed from Day One be vindicated, and those who have gotten away with "mur- der" for years pay up. Hyenas giggle, but it's unlikely they appre- ciate *humor*—that they're really laughing at their own silliness the way sane humans can. Furthermore, I would add the human potential for *awe*, those moments that pull us up short and we say, "Wow!" and "Oh, my God!"

Where do we get those qualities if other animals don't have them to pass on?

FOR REFLECTION

Take care in answering this question before discussing it with your child or student. The care you give in answering this question will be a reliable indication of whether or not you think the God Question is, in fact, crucially important to your values.

At the moment, what evidence do you have to substantiate your belief or disbelief in a Mind-Behind-It-All from (1) first- hand experience, (2) common sense, (3) reason, and (4) testi- mony—not just from what believers and unbelievers say, but also what they do: from the quality of their lives?

5

THE AMERICAN DREAM

*Nothing is sufficient for the person who finds suffi-
ciency too little.*

—Epicurus

Pose the question about the understanding of the word *success*
with your teenager. Are your child's answers still "comfortably
vague"? This is an age when one decides how long one can delay
commitments, which by their nature curtail freedom. "Mom, I'll
get to it!...I'll get to that when I'm in college....When I get out
into the *real* world....When I get married...have kids...retire....
Surely, I'll get to that before I die!"

As for the genuine content of their understanding of success,
there's nothing culpable—or incurable—about your teenager
being acquisitive. We're all cousins of simians who (we assume)
naturally grab what they want when they want it. Moreover,
now every child has been scrupulously "trained" to acquire since
the first commercial they vaguely grasped. However, entertain
the possibility that all of us, not just the advertisers, but teachers and parents, have unknowingly connived in that training.
Isn't it true that the only effective motivation schools or parents
use about school is "You've got to get a good education or you'll
never get a decent, that is, *well-paying*, job." Or suppose your
child said one night after dinner, "Ya know, I've been so lucky;
I'd really like to spend my life giving back. I'd like to be a social
worker (or a special education teacher)." Would your first, unre-
flective response be "Wait a minute! How the hell much can you
make doing that?" That's a legitimate, caring question. Maybe
"man doesn't live by bread alone," but we can't live without it
either!

43

Hold your breath for this one! What if your child came home and said he or she wanted to be a priest or a nun? Would you, deep down, feel you'd somehow failed, and that all that tuition money had somehow been wasted?

The only brainwashing worthy of the name is the kind that you'd swear you'd never received. The materialist gospel has been so subtle, so constant, so seductive that we'd all swear we're unaffected by it. So why are its jingles rattling around our heads when we're not occupied? They don't spend $150 billion a year on it because it doesn't work. Furthermore, anyone who denies that it has been "good" for all of us is blind or a fool. None of us wants to go back trudging to the town well, or beating clothes on the rocks by the stream, or trekking to the outhouse.

The propaganda systems—the American Dream (embodied in the commercial media), pop culture, the institutional churches, formal schooling, and peers and parents—are all trying to sway your opinions on a most basic question: What will make you happy, fulfilled, and successful? In critiquing all five of these propaganda systems, a touchstone whose legitimacy most kids *will* accept is "good servants, bad masters." It's foolhardy—not to mention unjust—to condemn the Cyber Matrix out of hand, the way uneducated villagers burned witches who were simply practicing effective folk medicine. Capitalism is not the antichrist, any more than "the flesh is wicked." It just needs to be kept in check, lest it become a false god.

Another counterargument that is useful, simply because it's inescapably true, is the manifest failure of the lives of so many who have definitively *achieved* all the goals of the American Dream: Elvis Presley, Marilyn Monroe, Howard Hughes, Michael Jackson, Judy Garland, Robin Williams, and a host of others, who "had it all," but were so unhappy that they had to drug themselves to get away from life and finally killed themselves. True enough, we can quote an equally impressive parade of other people who had it all and seemed remarkably "at home" inside themselves *despite* a dog-eat-dog world: Bill Gates, Derek Jeter, Angelina Jolie, Warren Buffet, Bono, and Michael Bloomberg. However, it would be an interesting discussion to explore, even from the inadequate evidence of the newspapers, the different attitudes apparent in the lives of those very wealthy and revered people who quit on life and those who haven't.

One "hesitant" suggestion is to rent the movie of Paddy Chayefsky's *Network*, which is a biting satire that lays bare the pretensions of most public entertainment. The characters' fundamental motives are not to instruct, or even to entertain, but to manipulate: to make money and achieve the power to control its flow. My hesitation about viewing the film in its entirety is occasioned by one bedroom scene that will be too explicit for family viewing. However, thanks to the Internet, segments of the film are available. If you read together the plot summary on Wikipedia or some other source, then watch the segments together in the following suggested order: (1) "I'm Mad as Hell" (4:22); (2) "The World Is a Business" (4:44); (3) "It's the Individual" (2:45); and (4) "We're in a Lot of Trouble" (3:56), or you can simply view them yourselves and choose a better sequence. (The fact that commercials intrude even on these "free access" Internet segments is a hoot!)

FOR REFLECTION

These notes assume that this approach is probably different from that of your own religious education, which is worth pondering. Share the hesitations about religious commitment you had when you were their age. If you had none, have you had any since? Hesitation is a human virtue, and doubt is the healthy urge to find more satisfying answers.

To assess as honestly as you can how much the gospel of the American Dream has affected your own values, first think of a specific job you'd truly love but that would probably allow you and your family just to "get by"; then consider an offer for a mind-numbing job on an assembly line making, say, plastic flowers that squirt water in people's faces for $80,000. Now, which job would you take—and more important, why?

6

ESCAPING THE RAT RACE

Too much is at least as dehumanizing as too little.
—Frederick Franck

No one can blame young people for getting fed up with the whole schooling business, especially when the "paychecks" are so rare and seldom come with raises. Didn't we feel the same way? The problem is that so many today have such a totally groundless optimism. Young people have some idea—again, God knows whence—that the rest of their lives will be so much better: College will be exciting, and surely, they'll find jobs that are not only exhilarating but highly paid. All the lights on the Yellow Brick Road to Emerald City will turn green, even before they have to slow down for them. Good luck!

In the bottom of their hearts, they *know* that's as much a lie as most commercials. However, they want both: the real success and the false hopes that it will arrive without effort, just as they want to be both somebody *and* just like everybody else—which, understandably, leaves them torn and confused.

The long-range drawback of all that optimism and postponing decisions to start acting adult (self-motivated) is that they aren't just escaping the rat race, but avoiding "the facts of life." That phrase has long been a euphemism for facing the realities of sex, not only physical but psychological. Even if they have side-stepped the psychological aspects of sexual maturity, today most adolescents are as aware of the physical aspects of sex as only farm kids used to be.

Nevertheless, there are quite a few "facts of life" from which a surprising number of young people have been almost completely protected, just as the father of the Buddha tried to

46

protect his son so that he would choose a worldly life rather than a spiritual one (Google: The Four Sights). The facts of life that so many are denied today are those four truths about suffering: poverty, sickness, old age, and death; and now one other burden, at least for those who are born without trust funds: work.

Some students undergo burdens way in excess of tolerable—full-time classes *and* full-time jobs, sometimes with even a second part-time job—to the point they aren't humanly capable of attaining the learning for which they sacrifice so painfully. However, those aren't common. Fortunately, some have to work at least summers to help financially. That's all to the good.

What this chapter confronts is that unfocused—and unfounded—hope that complete freedom lies somewhere "out there." Very few don't harbor the impossible dream captured in offerings like *Ferris Bueller's Day Off*, *The Bachelorette*, and so many drunken buddy movies that present a world without consequences, which is realistically further off than Alpha Centauri.

Just as the media stoke up our animal acquisitiveness, they also heat up our animal libidos. Both are the least common denominator—a sure sell.

However, that's not all humans are—merely consumers and copulators. Something significant within us is left unsatisfied. There's a secret buildup here: we claim the satisfaction is God.

Without uprooting an essential hope in the future, it's important for parents and teachers to kill off that unrealizable *inevitability* of success, happiness, and fulfillment—whatever we've decided those mean. There are countless realities of which no human has ever or will ever be free, like the laws of physics, our own past mistakes, and the unwelcome agendas of others.

Maverick resistance to the saddle is natural at their age, but they're not just wild horses. Human puberty signals a dramatic departure from what continues to hold true for pampered pets. In fact, it's a fair assessment of their proximity to adulthood to examine the depth to which the indolent, self-referential animal is under personal control—"Mom, I'll *get* to it!"

Every human needs a break, but there's something wrong when youngsters are looking for a break from their breaks, like

petulant kids on a rainy Saturday. Is it unfair for anyone financially subsidized to say *any* incursion on freedom is "unfair"?
Most adults have come to an uneasy peace with reasons to work:
to support those I love, to have pride in myself, and to justify the
creature comforts I want to have. Other "grown-ups" *haven't*
become "adults." They grew up, but never matured. From the
outside, they live what appears to be a life of frustration, little
different from the unease they felt during their schooling, with
the lack of any justifying reason to keep the work from being
tedious and meaningless. Therefore, just as they did as high
school students, they feel the need to bust out of the harness on
Friday nights and let 'er rip!

It's worth pondering just what has to take place *within* an
individual to make the difference between the 24/7 serene life
and the haphazard life of frustration.

Cultivating twisted ideas of freedom in the young or allowing them to continue unchallenged has long-range consequences. Just as wall-to-wall stories about fiscal betrayals,
breaches of contract, the international financial debacle breed a
kind of universal low-grade mistrust (Little League Paranoia),
the insistence on our primal need for self-indulgence, coupled
with the equally unavoidable need to eat and provide, can lead
to a kind of universal low-grade bipolar week (Little League
Manic-Depression), in which life means dragging through five
tedious days in order to explode-and-recover for two days. Willy
Loman's feckless son, Biff, says in *Death of a Salesman*:

> Well, I spent six or seven years after high school try-
> ing to work myself up. Shipping clerk, salesman, busi-
> ness of one kind or another. And it's a measly manner
> of existence. To get on that subway on the hot morn-
> ings in summer. To devote your whole life to keeping
> stock, or making phone calls, or selling or buying. To
> suffer fifty weeks of the year for the sake of a two
> week vacation, when all you really desire is to be out-
> doors with your shirt off. And always to have to get
> ahead of the next fella. And still—that's how you
> build a future. (16)

As Peggy Lee sang, "Is that all there is?" Furthermore, if "the real me" is finally let loose by a few beers and some hot music and movement on Friday, what kept "the real me" locked inside all the work week?

So the crucial question is this: What is it that works inside the people who are (almost) as happy on their jobs all week as they are letting loose on the weekend? What's their secret? What could your youngster *inject* into the school week that would make it life-giving instead of a drag? Let's stick with that till we come up with at least a temporarily satisfying answer. Put the book aside. What will you tell them that will make their lives happy instead of five-sevenths drudgery? It could make all the difference, now...and forever!

The issue of crimping freedom isn't in any way restricted to sex. It also encroaches on work and on any other commitment that becomes inconvenient.

When I directed musicals, the accepted rule was that if you miss two rehearsals with no valid excuse, then you're out. On the sign-up sheet, that was clear in that the final statement was "I consider this a commitment," and the student signed his or her name. One year, I heard that three girls were going to skip the final and only weekend rehearsals in order to go on their senior ski trip. I called and asked each one not to do it. It was not that they were crucial, but I didn't want to cut them. I said, "You gave me your word." They denied it. "But you signed your *name*. That's *your* word." One girl started to cry, and her father grabbed the phone. "Listen, Father, you've got no business upsetting kids like that. She's going on the trip. They're only young once!" I asked him, "Is this ski trip more important than her word, her integrity?" He slammed down the phone.

On another occasion, one boy—one of only four boy dancers—dropped out a week before the show because "I'm not having fun anymore." Others got jobs, got into driver education "unexpectedly," got near-terminal detention. What is missing is perspective. Granted, the number of youngsters I dealt with at any one time was far larger than any parent could ever have, and some students in those plays went to lengths that were beyond-the-call to be there! Nevertheless, the propaganda works against commitment, which could be a reason why marriages are delayed or abandoned, and lifetime religious vocations have trickled away. "I'm with you forever...unless it stops being fun."

What's perhaps worse and more corrosive of happy lives is that kids believe that because they don't have lead roles, their presence or absence is unimportant. That's lethal in the long run.

POP MUSIC

On a sabbatical, I asked myself what I knew nothing about and should know more about. So I spent about six weeks researching book after book by female psychiatrists about "women's ways of knowing." Then I realized that, despite all my years in "Teenager Country," I knew almost nothing about pop music. So I bought all those fanzines and read quite a few tediously serious books on the roots of its appeal. I confess I came out of that only marginally more insightful.

One chapter was entitled "Kurt Cobain Died for Our Sins." It was a swamp of hogwash that painted Cobain as a victim of "society"—an idea that appeals to young people who are straining to emerge from the control of their intrusive, but still necessary, parents. Cobain injected himself with three times the lethal dosage of heroin. He pulled the needle out of his arm, carefully put it with the other paraphernalia back into a cigar box, rolled down and buttoned his sleeves, then picked up a Remington 20-gauge shotgun, placed it in his mouth, and discharged it.

His suicide note shows that he was an intelligent, articulate young man. It is enlightening about his life perspective:

> The roar of the crowds begins, it doesn't affect me the way in which it did for Freddy Mercury....The worst crime I can think of would be to rip people off by faking it and pretending as if I'm having 100% fun....I'm too sensitive. I need to be slightly numb in order to regain the enthusiasms I once had as a child....I think I simply love people too much, so much that it makes

me feel too f***ing sad. The sad little, sensitive, unappreciative, Pisces, Jesus man. Why don't you just enjoy it? I don't know!...I can't stand the thought of Frances [his two-year-old daughter] becoming the miserable, self-destructive, death rocker that I've become....I'm too much of an erratic, moody baby! I don't have the passion anymore, and so remember, it's better to burn out than to fade away.

Peace, love, empathy,
Kurt Cobain

It would be a true learning experience to sit together with your child and go through that painful little essay, phrase by phrase, and try to tease out the self-deceptions.

FAKE FUN

Sometimes, I wonder about the wisdom of it, but I tell high school and college students that I have tried smoking grass twice. The first time, I had smoked cigarettes so much that nothing "happened." The second time, I was with some wealthy folks on a beach. The first time the pipe went around, nothing happened. Then, the second time it was, "One for you, one for Bill, one for you, one for Bill...." I ended up howling with laughter. But there was nothing funny.

It was exactly like being tickled, which little kids may enjoy, but adults don't. It wasn't a *human* reaction, just a physical one. With both the marijuana and the tickling, I was passive; a nerve was stimulated, and I reacted with no more personal involvement than Pavlov's dog salivating at the sound of a bell. The ability to laugh and have fun is always "in there someplace," but even in my diddled state, I felt somehow cheated. Hoaxed! I'd taken something fake for real.

Then I saw one of the group heading toward the surf, and somewhere inside my fuzzy, befuddled mind I said, "In the state he's in, he could walk in and drown." And I didn't care.

That's when I became certain I never wanted to blow grass again.

Even though you may not know Greek, it's worth drawing the connection between "narcissism" (self-centeredness) and "narcotics." The Greek root is *narkoun*, which means "to benumb." Hypnotic chemicals *divorce* us from reality, which is quite likely why the famous folks who overdosed even began on that path. Life-as-it's-delivered was simply too overpowering for them. They couldn't handle it. Why? Because they'd never achieved the natural goal of adolescence, which is to find and accept a personally validated self: an identity, a Who-I-Really-Am.

Perhaps most adolescents who ever lived just "waited for adulthood to happen," all by itself, the way grown-up-hood happened, without any input or effort from the individual. However, Fairy Godmothers exist only in fairy tales and Disney movies. Most of the oldest folk tales about becoming a true adult involve working your way through some kind of "hell" and coming out the other end with your dignity intact. Think of *Lord of the Rings* and *The Wizard of Oz.*

Becoming an adult human can't occur for those who cling to any kind of dependency that short-circuits their need for effort to face life on life's terms. The body *naturally* builds up a tolerance for the substitutes, which in turn demands a stronger dosage...and on it goes. This does not mean that one puff of grass leads inevitably to a heroin overdose, but it's a first step, without which the overdose is highly unlikely.

Ironically, more than the danger of physical addiction, dependence on *any* substance—drugs, food, booze, and sex—is tragically a surrender of ownership of *oneself.* There's a motivation that does get through to the young. Every child, despite the yearning to belong and not to be excluded, wants just as intensely to be *somebody*, not to be negligible.

You simply can't be somebody and exactly like everybody else. It's impossible and frustrating!

Good servants; bad masters.

FOR REFLECTION

Think of one person you know who is really proud of his or her job—not that it is "important" in a material sense, but one that he or she really is excited about, can't wait till Monday morning for, doesn't need any anesthesia to forget about. What is the job? What is it about the job that makes this person super-alive? In what concrete, specific ways can you see and feel that person's enthusiasm about his or her job?

Now think of your own learning. How could you make your job super-alive?

7

THE IMPERFECT CHURCH

All the boats leak. But the Catholic Church seems to leak least.

—Wally Kuhn

Those who try to elicit a genuine interest in the Catholic approach to God need to be intensely aware that adolescents' *experiences* of the Church are the biggest obstacle to the Church. Furthermore, it is also one of the major blocks to a fair consideration of God, with whom the Church is often misidentified, as if the flaws of the latter are reflected in the Other.

The resistance comes not just from the recent scandals or, closer to every week, the disaffecting liturgy, but also the overkill of religious head-trip instruction that's taken place since your children were first introduced to religion. The Church's propaganda was, in the first place, not as incessant as the "world's" propaganda. What's more, the world's propaganda is far more professionally executed—written, acted, directed, and artfully displayed by the finest talents money can buy—unlike those who produce and deliver the Catholic message. Moreover, the world's message is a direct appeal to the least common denominator in all humans: the unregenerate id, the acquisitive and rapacious wolf that true civilizations have tried to tame since the caves—with mixed success. Worst of all, some realize that what we're purveying, once youngsters are old enough to deal with unpleasant realities, is an embodiment of God's will in a repellent crucified felon worn to death with serving ungrateful others.

Therefore, since Vatican II, a too-reckless understanding of the Council's welcome easements seems to have led to a defusing of the less appealing elements of the Christian message: sin and forgiveness, death and rebirth. (To be fair, the element of serving others is more vigorous now than ever.) However, in "domesticating" any demanding elements of Christianity, we've homogenized it into unappealing insipidity, and are left with "Moralistic Therapeutic Deism."

At least the crucifix stood as a challenge to innate youthful idealism, just like Glinda, Gandalf, Obi-Wan Kenobi, and Dumbledore. The pastel Jesus is easily dismissable.

Well-meaning religious educators have presented instead "placebo" Christianity, wherein "Jesus is my personal savior," who lugs away my embarrassing sins, even though confession lines have disappeared. The Good Shepherd watches over us and wants only to make our lives happy. Fine teachers who have had summer workshops in Scripture leave students at least with the impression that all those stories, like the stories of Paul Bunyan, are made up by primitive people and are nothing to worry about. As a result of this suppression of the up-and-at-'em Jesus, who went after the pharisees and the money changers and his own pupils, we have the expurgated Lamb of God. No wonder he's unappealing. Instead of being a threat to complacency, Jesus becomes a smiling irrelevance.

Soul Searching offers two interesting conclusions: First, the greatest influence shaping teenagers' beliefs is their parents; and second, that among all denominations, despite remarkable recent efforts like the *Catechism* and national *Syllabus*, Catholic youth are the most apathetic.*

By some very vague route, religion seems to dribble through young peoples' filters in a way that, even after all these years in the classroom, is simply difficult to grasp. Difficult to comprehend too is the content of what they *understand* of Catholicism's promises. They're more tolerant of "Christianity" than "Catholicism," and more likely to respond to "spirituality" than "religion." So it is here that I begin.

Their elusiveness about religion is possibly that there's not much substantive *there*. Too much of what they "took on board"

---

*Christian Smith and Melinda Lundquist Denton, *Soul Searching* (New York: Oxford University Press, 2009), 216.

were doctrines that were meaningful only to get a grade and have later been cleared out with the trash in the move to high school or college. However, even the more basic elements of *any* religion seem to have been dumped, or more likely never offered or clarified for minds moving beyond the cartoon simplicities of childhood.

Heaven still seems to be a thin hope-laced reality, but both hell and purgatory withered away long ago. Those simply cannot subsist with the all-loving God. In fact, I do not sense any awareness or acceptance of dimensions to reality beyond the here-and-now or very immediate future in reflections from either high school or college students. Both younger and older groups have utopian ideas of the next stage beyond schools, but, because they've been glutted with fake deaths and shielded from real deaths, I can intuit no sensitivity to a transcendent dimension to reality and human value. Having tested the waters in so many places and at so many levels, I don't believe my assessment is invalid, although it could be at least open to question. However, the Smith-Denton study lends strong support to my experience.

Disneyland delivers as promised in the ads. Even if you're a grump, you get seduced into having fun despite yourself. Do I have to tell anybody that the usual weekend Mass does *not*? If the performance is lackluster and the homily an endless circular bore, then the Mass is an actual test of faith. If the Mass is repellant, then so is the Church, so is religion, and so is God.

Start from where they are, or you're just spinning your wheels. The more you try to promote religion as a value in the face of, on one side, the far more appealing voices of the other happiness propaganda *and*, on the other side, the repugnance at both the Church's "product" and its "sales pitch," you are not only eroding your own credibility, but causing a continual reinforcement of your students' or your children's rejection of it.

A MIDDLE ROAD

Earlier, I unfairly simplified. Those who hold back on the meaning of the crucifix aren't wrong. They just seem to hold off on it for too long, as with almost all other challenges to childhood. What I suggest for *post*-children is a middle road between Jesus in agony and Jesus the Warm Fuzzy. On the one hand, genuine Christianity is not a gathering of those Spanish *penitentes* whipping one another through the streets that TV usually shows around Holy Week. However, on the other extreme, the Church is not a benevolent association like the Lions Club or Junior League.

Those too prevalent but painfully inadequate understandings are a large part of why many young people find religion so dismissible. Remember the prototypical Goldilocks: "This one is too hard. This one is too soft. This one is just right." Despite overpampering and misdirections from the media, the natural adolescent hunger for a heroic life isn't entirely smothered. Furthermore, even though formal catechesis overlooks the need to reignite that urge, the very first converts to the gospel seem not to have been won over by *doctrine*—even by what came to be the most potent one: the resurrection. What lured them was the vibrant, confident, magnetic *person* of Jesus and the effect that charismatic person had on those bringing them the message. Now, those bringing them that combustive challenge is...us.

As the later chapter on Christianity will do more thoroughly, try treating Jesus accessibly—not the pale, wispy holy card, but a big man with carpenter's fingers. Somebody like the actor Hugh Jackman, who *projects* appeal to both males and females just by the way he carries himself. It would be a great inducement if one or both parents went through the Gospels and bracketed places where the Jesus they've come to admire over the years stands out—probably because of what he spoke or how he acted. It has nothing to do with "doctrines." Examine what kind of *man* would speak that way, respond to others' weaknesses that way, and go looking for the lost and bewildered that way. Save "the God part" at least for a while. Jesus did that, didn't he?

Stay on that level, at least until tenth grade, when reason starts simmering in there. That should take quite some time. The new official *Syllabus* begins with Jesus as our model, presuming that, because Jesus objectively *is* God's model for us, every sane person *ought* to value Jesus as a personal model. While that would be nice, it's so unrealistic.

First, it's counterproductive to say outright, "Jesus is our model." That's as unwelcome as asking, "Why can't you get good grades like So-and-So?" or "Why can't you be well-mannered like...?" Deadly! Furthermore, even though they *do* have a hunger for heroes, just as they have a hunger for God and for better than this life, you can't presume they *know* that. Keep in mind *salesmanship*: every good salesperson develops in the customer an awareness of what they really *need* but don't feel it yet. Help them *feel* the need.

In the past ten years or so, when I hand out a half-sheet asking whom students admire in contemporary life, at least half leave that line blank or write, "I have no heroes." That's understandable, isn't it? When checkout line tabloids have teams on every prominent person, reporting every foible and misstep, with no need to identify them beyond their first names—"Brad and Angelina to part ways"; "Suri is engaged"; "Brittney tops two hundred pounds"—how can heroes even exist when every candidate has had his or her Achilles' heels and Electra complexes published? Hero worship is too great a risk for today's young. (This may be the first time in human history that's true.)

Can you think of someone today in public life admirable beyond their skills at boys' games or making money or playing acoustic guitar? By the time this hits print, Derek Jeter will have retired. Oprah Winfrey? Bill and Melinda Gates? However, could anyone achieve notoriety and admiration for teaching impaired kids or running soup kitchens on a more than stop-in-for-a-photo-op basis? Toward the end of Mother Teresa's life, there was a rush to give evidence of how testy and demanding she was. In effect, how impossible virtue is to maintain.

I'm sure I sound close to cynical, but I speak for our real religious education audience.

Just as students have deflated the claims of their schools since the beginning, so this book tries to expose the dramatic shortcomings of propagandists they've accepted without criticism. Simple common sense ought to tell parents and teachers that before you present theology, that is, faith seeking understanding, we can't proceed until the audience is *ready* to be *converted.*

Conversion means a total turnaround. When Jesus said, "If you want the first place, take the last place," he was saying far more than "Put others ahead of you"—although, he did mean that, too. He was saying, "*Stop* in your tracks!" There are *two* races heading diametrically in the opposite direction from one another. There's the James Bond race: Aston-Martin cars, effortless ingenuity, an unbroken record of conquests in combat and bedroom, ingeniously lethal toys, flawless clothes, manners, and grooming; and there's the Jesus race: "How can I help you?...Thanks, I really have more than I need....No, you go ahead; I can get a later one."

These conflicting pairs of dynamisms do not mean you judge yourself—your worth, your life, yourself—by *being* James or Jesus. The only discriminant is in which of the two directions your sincerest heart is heading right now.

Once again, I suggest that conversion can never happen by itself. Someone has to help. Nor do I believe that *seismic* reversal of values can occur in young people who have been "shielded from harm and given the best we can." If the core of the gospel is forgiveness and resurrection from death, it can never even graze the fortifications against it within even the best-hearted young people, who've been told that guilt trips are bad for them and have seen death trivialized and even negated. Refrigerators for Eskimos, hockey skates for Bedouins.

REASONS I STAY

What follows asks teachers and parents to take on the more difficult—and far more persuasive—task of offering their own heartfelt motives for remaining Catholic Christians. These are mine.

It was Jesus whose forceful *presence* worked the turnabout in his first apostles and disciples. Since then, every Christian has been drawn not by a catalog of doctrines, but by the conviction of some believer previously brought to faith by yet another believer.

1. I would be a hypocrite to say I believe in a Creator to whom I owe everything but fail to *show* intense gratitude.

2. Consequently, if a "connection" to God is a matter of honorable gratitude, I need "a" religion. It needn't be an organized religion, but I must have a way to express *my* connection.

3. Having checked out all the religions possible (they're all right there on Google), Christianity appeals the most (cf. Goldilocks). The reasons:
   a. It welcomes me back, no matter what.
   b. Someone has a purpose for suffering, even if I don't know what that is.
   c. It promises that my inner self will survive death and is not negligible.
   d. I feel a need not to be alone in my belief, therefore I need other believers.
   e. Jesus' view of life's purpose "feels right."
   f. Maybe the clincher: of all the religions/connections to God I've studied, only Christianity's God has suffered and was tempted to despair, as I have.

4. For all its imperfections, past and present, Catholic Christianity seems the least leaky Christian boat.
   a. All others broke away from the Roman original, often for valid reasons.

b. The Catholic Church has weathered continual attacks from without and corruptions from within for twenty centuries, longer than any other institution in history, which is some kind of miracle.

c. No matter how dull or irritating a particular act of worship is, I trust that a miracle is going on underneath it. I trust that as confidently as I trust science when it says a rock is not really solid, or when medicine says my stomach ache is caused by gas and not cancer, or when someone says, "And I love you, too."

d. I feel perfectly safe in disagreeing with the official Church without fear of being a heretic or a traitor. For a while, Peter, the very first pope, was an apostate—within only hours of his ordination and first Mass.

Viva Goldilocks!

FOR REFLECTION

There is no need to rehash the obstacles outside yourself; the chapter has been pretty forthright about those. What are the obstacles *inside* yourself, as an individual, to giving the Church an open-minded chance to make its case? What are the specific biases that at least might be baseless—and therefore worth reconsidering?

8

THE IMPERFECT SCHOOL

Whoever has a why to live for can put up with almost any how.
—Friedrich Nietzsche

For years, I've taken inordinate pleasure teaching this topic. Every time, the astonished looks on students' faces show conclusively that this is the first time, ever, anyone's dared to ask, "Why have you been *doing* all this 'stuff' for so long?" Furthermore, it's being asked by a guy who, no doubt, has been inflicting it on young people for most of his life! They may not think to pose the question, but they have to have been wondering in an unfocused way why grown-ups never seem to find use for all the things inflicted on their children: Shakespeare, quadratics, and Latin.

No one seems to have thought that the work would be so much less tedious if students had been given a *why* to justify it; a meaningful *reason*. The only one that holds any effective motivation recently is the alleged connection between the schooling process and the avoidance of abject poverty, as if recognition of a trapezoid or the speaker of "to be or not to be" were a vaccination against the loss of all one's toys.

The reason students are so crestfallen when I broach this class is that I'm pulling out from under them the only support they've accepted for enduring sixteen years of servitude: "You need a good education in order to get a good, that is, well-paying, job." I'm surprised that the folks who already provide shrewd (and subsidized) students with fake term papers—without fear of jail time—haven't found a way to provide fake high school transcripts. It hardly seems difficult. Furthermore, it's only one step below helping well-to-do kids outfox the SATs and, in so doing, outsmart the entire purpose of the school system. Information outweighs thinking skills.

If all of us can keep being painfully honest, do most parents who pay tuition for schools that are free to use *Meeting the Living God* do so primarily because they inculcate values like those of the Sermon on the Mount or, more realistically, because the discipline and expectations are more demanding; because they are a more reliable preparation for college and a good job? Those are hardly motives to be ashamed of. However, if Shakespeare and calculus are unnecessary for success in academia and the marketplace, far less could be said for the utility of a "God" course. At least other courses are reputed to help one make a living; all a religion course can do is open the question of what living is *for*.

Once children have mastered basic literacy and computational skills (and a reliable self-control), they have the rudiments of what so many fabulously successful and world-changing individuals managed to get on their own without the help of professional educators: Harry Truman and seven other presidents, the Wright Brothers, Adolf Hitler, George Eastman (Kodak), George Bernard Shaw, Albert Einstein, Frank Lloyd Wright, Winston Churchill, John D. Rockefeller, Ted Turner, Roy Kroc (McDonald's), Marlon Brando, Maurice Sendak, Dave Thomas (Wendy's), Robert DeNiro, Peter Jackson (*Lord of the Rings*), Stan Lee (Marvel), Simon Cowell, Walt Disney, Bruce Springsteen, and others. Furthermore, if the students haven't been too much "trouble" to the institution, it will offer them a diploma certifying those achievements. What that list of names testifies to is the overkill imposed by four more years of the same, with greater intensity, and at a staggeringly more demanding financial expense—*provided* they have interiorized the four Ds: Discipline, Drive, Determination, and a Dream.

They don't need any more knowledge, any more information. They need to remember *nothing* of what they heard in class. That's at their fingertips on Google. However, if they haven't learned to be curious, humble in following where the evidence leads, able to reason clearly and honestly, responsible for themselves and others, and confident in their ideals and their skills, by the time they're eighteen, it seems naïve to think four more years will ignite those habits. We might as well hope that the Fairy Godmother appears in June of senior year of college, goes "*Ping!*" on their foreheads with her golden wand, and infuses the four Ds just in time before graduation.

Once students have the critical, fundamental skills of reading, writing, and 'rithmatic, their goal should then be learning how to *reason* to trustworthy personal decisions: gather, sift, outline, conclude, critique, with increasingly more complex problems and situations. That's what they'll need when their boss says, "By Friday, I want your best recommendation for that Jones business." They won't have to wait until March of their senior year college to say, "What am I gonna do now that Welfare has dried up?" If they waited that long, then they'll have to take whatever they can grab. However, if they've learned how to reason, they won't have to bedevil their friends with questions like "Are you sure you think he/she's the right one to marry? Can we afford a child? Is a house worth a mortgage? What are we gonna do about Mom and Dad?"

No matter whether they can no longer remember how to find the tangent of angle AOC or list five factors that precipitated World War I, if they've learned the skills to reason, it won't matter if all the cops in the world went on strike. They can figure out the right thing to do. Think back to all the problems that were unheard of when you yourself were in high school: the end of the Cold War and Apartheid, home computers, the Internet, cell phones, radical Islamic terrorism, extra-vaginal conception, genetic engineering, and the economic meltdown. We relied on TV commentators not only to tell us that those things had occurred but, more or less, how we ought to evaluate them, how to make *sense* of them. If your children have learned how to think clearly and honestly, they won't need the *Catechism*, or even the Ten Commandments.

To show kids that thinking can be exhilarating and fun, play Twenty Questions with them on endless car trips. Google sites that offer riddles (and the answers) like the following:

1. A man was found dead in an open field, no one was around, but an unopened package. (The package was a parachute.)
2. What is greater than God, more evil than the devil, the poor have it, the rich need it, and if you eat it, you'll die? (Nothing.)
3. Which creature walks on four legs in the morning, two legs in the afternoon, and three legs in the evening? (A human being—the third is a cane.)
4. What can travel around the world without leaving its corner? (A stamp.)
5. What is the only word in English that is *always* misspelled? ("misspelled.")
6. Feed me and I live. Give me a drink and I die. What am I?
7. A man is pushing his car along the road when he comes to a hotel. He shouts, "I'm bankrupt!" Why?
8. How many of each species did Moses take on the ark with him?
9. He has married many women, but has never been married. Who is he?
10. What invention lets you look right through a wall?

What did you feel inside reading the latter five riddles that you didn't feel reading the first five? *The itch of curiosity.* Unlike math texts, you can't turn to the back of the book to relieve yourself of the need to think. In fact, when you're playing with a riddle, the best way to ruin the game is for someone who's heard it before to blurt out the answer! Catechisms and doctrinal instructions give you the answers. Genuine religious exploration infects you with puzzlement that can lead to true learning. Maybe even a personal connection to God! Answers can never make that happen. [(6) Fire, (7) Monopoly, (8) Noah, (9) a priest, (10) a window.]

All the great teachers who ever lived didn't *transport* their favorites to fulfillment. They made them, by God, *work* for it!: Socrates, Aesop, Mohammed, Booker T. Washington, John

Dewey, John Thomas Scopes, Annie Sullivan, Maria Montessori, Jaime Escalante.

Jesus never explained the Trinity. He simply dumped the facts in the laps of his followers and drew them hither and yonder for a couple hundred years before they came up with even just a "moderately satisfying" answer. He only once dissected a parable (The Sower). The rest were all metaphors they had to unpack and reinfuse with life for themselves—banquet, treasure in a field, eye of a needle, seed, leaven, fish net, bridesmaids, and the footrace. Of course, not really that much later, "experts" arose who, unarguably, had more education and skills at interpretation, and who willingly took over and relieved nearly everybody else of the burden of learning for themselves. Stuff them with the answers, and then leave them to till their fields and bake their bread. Really bad teaching! Instead, Mao said, "Teach them how to fish." While they differed radically on some crucial viewpoints, for sure, both Jesus and Mao knew their audience. They were down-to-earth, practical men.

FOR REFLECTION

Write out, for yourself, what kind of *why* you hope your children would freely choose to help them get through any unbearable *how*.

9

PARENTS AND PEERS

The weak are more likely to make the strong weak than the strong are likely to make the weak strong.
—Marlene Dietrich

The age-old wisdom at the heart of *Hansel and Gretel* is that, sooner or later, painful as it may seem to both sides, children must be booted from the nest—even with a chance they're gobbled up by bears or meet with foul-tempered witches with the same intentions. In "the natural order of things," they have to learn to fend for themselves, using their own wits and spunk.

However, for a long while, it's precarious and scary being "out there on your own." Your human nature impels you to become an independent "somebody," relevant, a "self." Yet, at the very same time, you yearn for the warmth, support, and "belonging" that have come mostly from parents and family. I suspect that not many parents or teachers help children face the dilemma of wanting to stand alone, singular, and yet not stand out as odd, singular. It's a painful polar tension.

Young people have to exercise the same critical intelligence about opinions that come from their own parents and pals as we'd like them to exert in regard to media, counterculture, schooling—even religious schooling. That's an integral, but usually ill-served, goal of becoming an adult.

PARENTS

Parental influence on their children's ideas and ideals began only slightly ahead of the influence of the electronic babysitter. It was less professional, but it was reinforced by love, loyalty, forgiveness, shared experience, and gratitude. As the chapter suggests, when parents give advice based on concrete personal experience of mistakes and consequences, they're almost invariably right, no matter how constricting the rules their experience forges and enforces. However, when parents talk about theory—values, behavior, religion, social policy— then, with grateful respect, their young ought to subject those opinions to adult scrutiny.

When I get counterarguments in class, for instance about Welfare, homosexuals, Iraq, immigration, capitalism, I'm almost never talking to the student. I'm talking to his or her father, who has to face the burden of taxes. Students' "personal" opinions aren't something they researched in any meaningful way. And quite often neither has the parent. However, the loyal conviction behind the opinion often provokes a gnashing of teeth when it's challenged, as if a contrary opinion is a personal attack against the intelligence and character of their father or mother.

At the two ends of the spectrum of responses to adults' opinions, there is, at one end, a complete unquestioning subservience, and at the other, a relentless skepticism looking for soft spots for debate. Every child sits somewhere in between. Probably the uncritical stance, strictly loyal to the parents' opinion, is rarer now, but is most difficult to crack, simply because it's so enmeshed in positive values like love and loyalty. It takes a confident parent or teacher to say, "It's okay to challenge me, really, as long as you do it politely. Your bosses and colleagues will respect you more if you do have the courage to think for yourself and the confidence to differ." Any teacher can tell within a week the students who have been encouraged to pitch into a discussion with assurance at home. The most painful classes can be those where kids are fearful that any threat to their *opinions* is a threat to *them* ("Are you callin' me a moron?").

The first lesson for a parent is that no issue—no argument whatever—is worth more than the loving between parent and child. Being more experienced, the adult has the burden of shucking off the bruised feelings first and saying, "Hey! This is outta hand. Can I have a hug?"

The second lesson for a parent is to school oneself to hear the objections and resistances from their child's point of view, with *their* ears. They're just starting, first, to have an independent point of view; second, to smell rats even in the most "settled" areas; and third, to paw through an insufficient vocabulary to say exactly what they mean. In most cases, each of us has fumbled and bumbled around until we finally stumble into a more or less serviceable set of thinking and speaking skills. If only the schools could pull back and accept that the *content* of their particular disciplines and syllabi is in no way as critical as leading young people to learn how to think.

The basic attitude of the truly humble—and helpful—parent is "Help me understand what *you* really mean. *Then* we can talk."

Another skill, which is of great need "out in the real world," is one that I've never heard taught, or that I have emphasized myself. It is the essential skill of sizing up the person you have differences with and accepting the prudent conclusion that any further argument will be utterly wasted; that all the argument is doing is riling tempers and building resentments. That's a place where the left brain's need not to lose has to yield to the right brain's hunch that this is not looking for truth, but rather for dominance. Sometimes, the shrewdest comment is "Hey! Let's not talk about this anymore, okay?" It's like stepping into a fistfight between little kids, where it leaves both sides steaming and frustrated. However, that beats atomic war. "Let there be peace on earth, and let it begin with me."

PEERS

Who cares about the opinions of shallow boors? Most of us.

—Victor Steele

It's quite common that when youngsters "unplug" the default opinions they'd assumed from their parents, the experience is so unnerving that they quickly "plug in" the unspoken, often merely imagined, opinions of the particular kids they settle in with, usually like Goldilocks, with no logic involved. They cluster more by the accident of being lumped together by schedules, alphabet, extracurricular activities, and detentions—simply intuitive "mutual resonance."

Since conformity is always easier than thinking, a great many are willing to pay just about any reasonable price in order to be accepted, or at least not be rejected. Therefore, one's taste in music, clothes, and attitude warp readily into the "folk wisdom" of one's time and place. There is no real harm in that, but the shaky part comes when this new "society's" rules and customs verge into more serious areas than mere taste: drinking, drugs, fighting, and at least the pretense of being sexually active. Many peer judgments can be softened by a steady boy–girl *relationship*—a word that covers the gamut of possible involvement. Some steady connections are more rigidly monogamous, and self-impoverishing, than most marriages.

Teachers and discipline-folks can readily sense the tentacles connecting the "troublemakers." Anyone who proctors a cafeteria knows the soccer players, the yearbook kids, and the play kids. The ones those in charge should be most intensely aware of are the loners. However, one group, or perhaps subgroup of the others, is the one that reinforces one another's distaste for schoolwork and their cunning methods of eluding it. Those students need someone who can find ways to give them at least a mild jolt into doing something gratifying. Very often art class will do just that!

"Oh, Mom! *Everybody* does it!" In this case, try the absurd: "If everybody shaved their heads or shed their clothes or painted their faces blue?" Careful, though, because that might sound tempting to some.

A wise parent, no matter how otherwise busy, makes his or her youngster invite his friends over to the house. It's not spying, any more than reading a report card or attending their games and plays or going to a PTA meeting. If you have hesitations about your first surface impressions of the friends, for God's sake (literally), don't say, "I simply can't figure what you *see* in So-and-So," much less, "I don't want you hanging around

with those kids." Be humbler, more the friend than the precep-
tor: "So-and-So seems...?"—and there's a test of *your* vocabulary!—"Creepy, brassy, dim-witted?" Well, no.

VULNERABILITY, AGAIN

Just like when I tell the story of my reluctant squiring of
Catherine Cronin to her senior prom or that of my total self-
detestation over mediocre grades, I know that I have the students' undivided attention. In both cases, with apologies to
Ms. Dietrich, the reason is that it's the first time most of them
ever had an adult let down his guard, his reassuring projection
of somebody who's "got a handle on everything." Of course, we
can't do that too often, but if the admission comes from a person they've come to regard as "solid," confident, and reliable, it
doesn't weaken our persuasiveness, but strengthens it.

Such occasional admissions beat the daylights out of stories about holes-in-the-shoes and school treks uphill in both
directions, which ennoble the speaker rather than make him or
her more approachable and less susceptible to being imitated.
Additionally, they don't want to hear so much about how down
and out you were. What they want and need to know is how you
got yourself turned around.

A critical distinction lies between "respect" and "praise."
Every human being deserves respect; praise you have to earn. As
Eleanor Roosevelt insisted, "No one degrades you without your
cooperation." However, as the essayist Joseph Addison wrote,
"In doing what we ought to do, we deserve no praise, because it
is our duty."

However, like *guilt, duty* is no longer a popular word. And
a good number of young people react with the sensitivity of sun-
bathers to the thinnest cloud if something seems to intrude
between them and idyllic freedom. Consider all those highly
successful suicides when young people discovered that "everything" simply wasn't enough. What teachers and parents owe
adolescents and young adults is facilitating their discovery of a
personally validated self, an identity within whom they can face

71

the world, not in some fantasy, but within the ways the world presents itself.

In *A Man for All Seasons*, Robert Bolt shows how St. Thomas More believed that the value of the individual soul is beyond price, yet the personal cost to maintain its integrity is heavy. Henry VIII commanded every citizen to take an oath accepting him as a worthier head of Christendom in England than the pope. Despite sanctions of treason, prison, and death, More's conscience refuses. He won't deny the claim, but he refuses the oath. His reason: "I will not give in because I oppose it—*I* do—not my pride, not my spleen, nor any of my appetites, but *I* do—*I!*" (Act II).

Martin Luther King Jr. said, "If you haven't found something in life worth dying for, you aren't fit to be living." Our task is not just to invite the young to have ideals worth dying for, but worth living for, worth defending, and passing on.

In *J.B.*, his modernized verse play on the Book of Job, Archibald MacLeish imagines Job's three comforters: a communist, who argues that his suffering is nothing within the massive movement of human history; a psychiatrist, who insists that Job's irrational search for answers is meaningless, since his soul is the helpless victim of his subconscious animal urges and the uncontrollable movement of events outside him; and finally a puritan cleric, who insists that Job was born human, an inheritor of original sin, thus corrupt beyond his ability to rectify that. Job responds in fury:

> I'd rather suffer
> Every unspeakable suffering God sends
> Knowing it was I that suffered,
> I that earned the need to suffer,
> I that acted, I that chose
> Than wash my hands with yours in that
> Defiling innocence. Can we be men
> And make an irresponsible ignorance
> Responsible for everything?
> I will not listen to you.

Before you deal with the subject of self-possession and integrity, it might help to Google chapter 17 of Aldous Huxley's *Brave New World* entitled "The Right to Be Unhappy," which argues that the utopias we crave so profoundly are dehumanizing; getting rid of everything unpleasant instead of learning to put up with it. Huxley's Savage, raised outside the smothering Utopia and who resists brainwashing into happiness, says, "What you need is something with tears for a change. Nothing costs enough here."

Huxley was a true prophet.

FOR REFLECTION

In no particular order, list the do's and don'ts you impose on your children or students. When you finish the list, go back and—without any self-deceptions—after each rejection, state your honest reason(s) for finding those rules justified. Then, give the list to someone whose breadth of perspective and honest judgments you trust. Ask for an honest critique of your reasons.

10

WHAT MAKES HUMANS HAPPY?

When one door of happiness closes, another opens; but often we look so long at the closed door that we do not see the one which has been opened for us.
                                                                    —*Helen Keller*

This chapter deals, in an unavoidably superficial way, with the core purpose of your children's adolescence: finding an identity. Without getting tangled in too much research, some readers may want to do an introductory search for Internet entries on Jean Piaget, Erik Erikson, and Bruno Bettelheim on the developmental psychology of adolescents—remembering always that even Freud believed that the essential element in a human being was not the mind but the *soul*.* Many school systems stop far short of that belief.

The story of the retriever, exhausted but wanting more of what she was born to do, tries to shake kids up a bit, and gets them to open their eyes and look at life's alternatives, rather than merely hopping aboard a treadmill in kindergarten, jumping to another treadmill for middle school, moving to another for high school, and then bound off onto yet another—each time at increasingly intimidating expense. If you were to ask at each stage, although no one does, "Why am I submitting to this process?" the almost invariable answer would be "Everybody has to." In fact, I have little doubt that few parents would have a more substantial reason. It's no more questionable than whether we should wear clothes.

"It's to prepare you for life."

---

*Bruno Bettleheim, "Freud and the Soul," *The New Yorker*, March 1, 1982.

74

What in heaven's name does *that* mean? How does this process *do* that?

Compulsory schooling was never intended merely to guarantee employers workers who could add up a balance sheet, read a blueprint, or make change at a cash register. The Founding Fathers of just about every society wanted worthy citizens, equipped with all of what eventually became the Scout virtues: Trustworthy, Loyal, Helpful, Friendly, Courteous, Kind, Obedient, Cheerful, Thrifty, Brave, Clean, and Reverent. They hoped for moral, God-fearing citizens. However, today, in an ethos that vaunts Lady Gaga, Charlie Sheen, Tiger Woods, Britney Spears, Justin Bieber, and Simon Cowell, it might be less easy to find young men and women who still find those twelve unbankable qualities appealing—or at least admit to it.

So far, the text has tried to deflate the pretensions of those adversarial propaganda. Now, it offers a more positive approach, beginning with the truths libraries have preserved for centuries about what *every* human being needs to do to fulfill his or her inborn potential, suggesting a more individual self-assessment, before the flight from the nest.

THE HUMAN SELF

The earlier exercise about the four objects of ascending inner value—rock, apple, stuffed bear, human doll—is obviously critical. The truth is anchored "out there" and will reveal itself to anyone patient enough to be led by its evidence. So far, that lesson has been pointed toward triggering the humility necessary to apprehend *any* truth—ultimately the God truths. However, we are still abrading the misapprehension, common to most graduate schools, for teachers to guarantee that "the student will *master* the data"—an approach that garners only information, like a pawnshop. It prepares contestants for *Jeopardy!*

The resistance to think beyond the *Syllabus* and its prefab answers is deep-seated. Even with college students, after I've done the four-species differences, *twice*, it's still difficult.

When I hold up my keys and say, "What are these, and how do you know what they're for?" of course, they snap off the perfectly obvious responses, and the only answer they can, but when I ask, "What *indicates* what they're for?" the answers are tissue-thin: "Everybody knows" or "You try them in a lock." Every time, it takes me at least twenty minutes to get someone to respond, "By the way they're *made!?*" The saw-teeth tell you they're keys—the same way the hard rock, the juicy apple, the alert bear cub, and the jabbering baby doll inform you what they are for.

What are the qualities that clearly differentiate the bear and the baby? Their *potential* within. The bear will grow bigger, but it is stuck with the faculties it began with. However, the child—any human child, including yours—has the potential to become at one end of the human spectrum Nelson Mandela, Mother Teresa, Abraham Lincoln, or Madame Curie, or at the other end, just over the line from other beasts, a drug pusher, a slaver, a gangbanger.

Our purpose is to lure them out onto that spectrum, and theirs is to move further along it.

How do we achieve this? The qualities that specify our species are that we can know, love, and grow more intensely human. These qualities are what we were born to do, just as rocks are meant to be available, vegetables are to feed us, and other animals are to help us achieve our God-given purpose. All are good servants, bad masters.

A crucial element *within* each species is that it *demands* more respect than that due to anything on the level below it. There's something objectively wrong—de-grading—in throwing oranges around in a cafeteria war, as if they had no more inner value than snowballs; something objectively wrong, or de-grading, in setting a live dog on fire, as if it had no more feelings than a log or a Christmas pudding. However, what degrades human beings?

Human beings are mistreated or abused if anyone treats a human as if it had no more dignity than an ox or a pound of liver or a stepping stone. Humans mistreat themselves when they avoid or resist opportunities to understand more, love more, and grow more intensely human. Our specifically different nature reveals that we are meant to edge further along that spectrum of humanity from our fellow animals, past bestial human beings like torturers or drive-by shooters, toward model human beings like Nelson Mandela and Joan of Arc.

The extent and quality of our knowing and loving is specifically different. It's not just awareness of isolated facts like other animals, but the ability to interlock them and move to understand. Furthermore, we can give not only instinctive affection, but self-sacrifice, even for those we can't stand at the moment. By working on that evolution, you'll be fulfilling your human purpose.

To test out the theory, ask your youngster to describe how they feel inside when they've let themselves become enslaved to senioritis or when for some time they've drifted along, doing the absolute minimum, squeaking by, beating the system. "Oh, it'll be so much better in college...when I get a job...when I get married." What does it *feel* like? Does it make you wag your tail with joy? If it makes you feel grim, snappish, dully angry, then it's quite likely not what you were made for.

Do *your* best with what you've *got*. That's fine! In the going, you're already *there*!

It's as simple as that! However, it will take a deal of patient persistence to make it attractive, memorable, and operative.

Pick someone from your own past who brimmed over with aliveness. In what concrete ways did it show? How did it stimulate *your* living? Share it with your youngster.

THE UNIQUE SELF

No textbook can do anything but wave in the general direction toward the next logical step: focusing on what makes this young person *unique*. Yet, that is the central task for any adolescent. Most of us probably fumbled around until we found a "self" that more-or-less didn't chafe too much, and very few had the help of psychological professionals.

If you feel the urge and the value, the Internet has various free personality tests, which some might find uncomfortable or even downright foolish. However, as long as you don't treat them like some kind of gypsy fortune teller or psychological pigeon-holes, they can be both fun and enlightening in focusing more directly a teenager's confused apprehension of who he or she is as a unique individual. Be sure that they keep in mind that the "game" is not "nailing" but "narrowing down," and making one's assets and liabilities less vague and confusing, and more honestly accessible to understanding. Two tests that seem harmless enough are "16 Personalities" and the "Enneagram Personality Test." Avoid the Scientology test, if only because it asks for mailing details.

Keep the metaphor of leaving the nest. Some young people's personalities get to that point as condors; some as sparrows. By the way they've reacted to all the prior influences of their lives, they're either extraverted or introverted. Neither is better; each has advantages and drawbacks. However, more important, unlike the birds, humans aren't frozen in those limits. We *can change*. Rather than having some vague dissatisfaction with themselves, it is an enormous help for kids to have a better focus on precisely what their less desirable habits are, so that they can start to mature.

Offering a little girl the choice between a fifty-dollar bill and her stuffed rabbit exposes three distinct-but-real estimations of *value*, which next to *love* is the most misused word in the language. The money has a real value. It has buying power, but the more sensitive kids will have seen that, to the little girl whose property, many forget, *is* the little girl's, the bill is probably as valueless as Monopoly money, which it would also be to an Australian Aborigine or a Martian. Those more sensitive will also see that, for the girl, the bunny has a value beyond the capacity of numbers, and destroying it would require a less-than-human response. However, although to most civilized people, the little girl is beyond even her evaluation of her toy, we can never escape the incursion on our ideas of "humanity" from the objective, persistent evidence of people and events like Nero, Genghis Khan, Attila the Hun, the Inquisition, the

Crusades, Hitler, Stalin, and all the out-of-work shopkeepers and housewives who were necessary to carrying out those men's inhumanities. Just as the capacity to be heroic is compacted within the potential of each human, so is that potential to be less than human, or beastly, or antihuman in ways no other beast could achieve. To ignore that is to deny children "the facts of life."

The reflection at the end of this chapter, which asks the student to locate him- or herself on the lines between the psychological extremes, is a temptation to know the unique self just a little better—to apprehend with more focus what the individual's "got goin' for ya."

The insights, for both parent and child, will be richer if the parent says, "Are you sure you're not being too hard on yourself?" —as would a good confessor or psychologist.

The Helen Keller story is, of course, the innermost core of this approach to the understanding of humanity and God. Lure them with the story, but make *them* formulate what truths Helen's story conveys. In class, I have them play "Trust," then discuss the gut fear of vulnerability, even when they fall back into the hands of their best friend. Low-level paranoia isn't the best starting point for faith either in friends or in God! Then I have them sit in a circle, eyes closed, trying to imagine being "safe" from outside intrusions, and I read them the abbreviated story of Helen Keller from *Meeting the Living God*, and then ask them to reach out and take the hands of the two persons on either side and ponder a few questions—with longish pauses: "What you have in your hands aren't just two pieces of meat but parts of two human beings. Everything that *is* each of those two people is present to you through that intrusive, embarrassing touch. Their parents think that they're the most precious things in the world. Is it possible you never really *noticed* either one? Like the hands of Helen's teacher, Annie, these hands are sending you messages. They're saying, 'I'm here. I'm just like you. This exercise is as uncomfortable for me as it is for you. I fear the *same* things. I long for the *same* things: to be noticed, to be cared about, to be loved.' How will this experience make you different...being with these two human beings tomorrow, next week?"

Finally, after a longer pause, I invite them to open their eyes and look at the two people—in a way that they'll know what color eyes they have tomorrow. Then, I ask them to shake hands with each of them and tell each other their names, even if they know them. Finally, before leaving the room, I get them to shake hands with everybody else in the class—with the same intensity.

They "get" the insight about how buttoned-up they are with one another.

FOR REFLECTION

As in the previous exercise, reflect with your student or child about whether you give God the same chance to "prove" himself.

Following are listed various qualities by which individuals differ, in a spectrum from one extreme to the other. Make an X that situates you on each spectrum. Then write a profile of yourself. It will be inadequate, of course, but a start.

introvert ....extravert
anti-intellectual ....intellectual
indifferent ....inquisitive
wary ....trusting
fluctuating..decisive
self-protective ....self-giving
discouraged...cheerful
resentful ....forgiving
worldly...spiritual
follower..leader

11

THE LIMITS OF LOGIC

What validates opinions? The subject is critical in approaching an understanding of what genuine faith means. In the first place, many—even well-educated professional church-folks— treat faith in God as if it were some "different breed of cat" from any other act of faith, as if faith in God were entirely conditioned on God's personal intervention to sanitize the recipient beforehand. It is true that many hold that "faith" is a *gift* from God. That is indeed true. However, a gift is not "imposed," just offered. It's up to the recipient to accept it freely or not. Like forgiveness, faith can't work if one feels no need of it. The goal of *Meeting the Living God* is to create that need.

Furthermore, many ultraconvinced Roman Catholics believe "*our* faith" is somehow specifically more refined, more virginal than the faith of other Christian denominations, and surely more purified than the faith of a pagan Aborigine.

Until warned otherwise, I take *faith* to be a word with the same content across the board, whether used in an adult baptism or in a wedding in which two people vow their faithfulness in a holy act of mutual trust. However, faith also happens in committing to a mortgage or sharing a secret. It encompasses any act of trust: going down into a subway, accepting a check, or taking the advice of your doctor or broker.

The biggest obstacle is misapprehension of what validates *reliable* faith. The subtlest terror an adolescent has is being embarrassed—being caught looking naïve or unsophisticated. On the one hand, there is the weak-minded suggestion that faith is a blind leap in the dark, which is sheer idiocy, and intelligent kids refuse to make that. On the other hand, some prefer "keeping an open mind" until evidence shows up that obliterates all hesitation and doubt, which is also impossible—and no one can provide that. Recall that every single eyewitness to Jesus' bodily resurrection held back belief—with the evidence right at his or her fingertips! When they finally *did* concede belief, it was *not* based on rational arguments found in a catechism.

Therefore, this approach has been probing the presently solidified convictions of our unique audience, exposing the fraud behind a great many of them, and encouraging them to a better foundation for those that are true but ill-substantiated. It's not unlike preparing your most *precious* possession, your child, to take out one of your most *expensive* possessions, your car. Surely, you'd never dream of handing over the keys before he or she was sure of the difference between brake and accelerator! Well, right here, you're preparing to transfer watchfulness and custody over their own souls.

For centuries, the official Church's approach to religious truths has been rigorously left brain and "academic." Even the prayers of the Mass betray the hands of theologians, historians, and liturgists, not poets. They have been far more "head" than "heart"—the inner self where "religion" takes place. Moreover, religious instruction has often been tragically *dualistic*, that is, division into irreducible binary oppositions. Complex realities are split handily into either/or bins, with no leakage or grey areas between good/evil, mind/body, male/female, and mortal/ venial. However, within the last century, science—especially insights into relativity and quantum physics—has made it unavoidable that reality defies such handy oversimplifications. For instance, an electron is *both* a solid pellet *and* a fluctuating wave at the same time! The formula $e = mc^2$ means that energy and mass are two forms of the *same* reality: energy (e) *is* mass (m) times the speed of light (c) squared. In psychology, we know that the male without the corrective of the once-stereotyped "feminine" values (empathy, contextual appraisal, yielding) is a brute and a female without the corrective of the once-stereotyped "masculine" virtues (clarity, confidence, decisiveness, assertiveness) is a doormat. The same is now true across the spectrum of values. Faith *without doubt* is fascism.

In order to discuss the need for *more* than honest logical reasoning or to ask whether your youngster is more of a strict utilitarian than a flexible altruist, offer him or her a hypothetical question. For example, suggest that you've got a transnational manufacturing company with ten small factories in minor cities across the country. Every one of them is perking along just fine, turning out a good product, good reception, and contented workers—except for the one factory in Boonyville. It's leaking red ink. Nothing has worked, including completely changing management and offering employees union incentives. You've tried everything you can. What's the only strictly *rational* decision? Of course, close it down; cut your losses, and move on.

However, as with the exercise with the little girl, the money, and the bunny, we hope that your child will hesitate. If he or she does, that could be a promising sign: "But wait a minute! What about the workers?" In this case, maybe your youngster has more than a cold, utilitarian understanding of human affairs. If not, then maybe you need to work on igniting one beyond the calculating mind.

"If your factory is the major income source in the area, what about peripheral businesses like dry cleaners and car repairs? If the tax base dries up, what happens to the schools?" The stereotypical, hard-nosed response to that objection is "We're not running a charity!"

If the socializing mechanisms have left your child with that attitude, I wouldn't hold out much hope for Christianity and the Sermon on the Mount. However, that objective attitude does seem to be the chilly, rational response when I do role-play hypotheticals in class. As one boy said, "These moral dilemmas are just the same as math problems—but with people."

The same is true of the certitudes from science classes that need merely to be asserted in order to be accepted. No salutary doubts. No? "Says who?" And we all yielded to it. Did anyone sneer when the teacher explained, way back in high school, that this table is not solid at all, but actually a hurricane of tiny pellets whizzing at such ferocious speeds that they only *seem* to be at rest—and most of it is empty space? They said that if you could magnify the two-element hydrogen atom to the size of the Astrodome, the nucleus would be a tiny piece of grit on the floor, the electron would be an even tinier grain up by the roof, and the rest would be...completely empty space.

Nobody objected, no more than they objected when another teacher talked about Socrates, and still another said if you mix ammonia and bleach you get chloroform and that inhaling the vapors could cause respiratory damage and throat burns. What's there to question? They've got professional degrees, they're state licensed, and they've got no motive to deceive me.

On the contrary, although the U.S. government has spent $140 million yearly for years to convince teenagers that unprotected sex is hazardous, there are still approximately 350,000 unwanted pregnancies per year. Furthermore, when you get to high school religious education classes, you'll get objections aplenty—especially from the really smart kids—when you say a clutch of people two thousand years ago came to believe that an alien presence arrived from beyond space/time in Palestine, lived the life of a carpenter-preacher, died, came back, and left a community of believers that's still flourishing. Right!

Why do they blithely swallow conclusions that baffle the clear evidence of their eyes and fingers on the mere declaration of an opinion from an educated scientist, but balk like ponies from fire at someone who claims religious expertise? Because physics and chemistry make almost no real incursions on a teenager's newfound freedom, but the unpleasant connection between sexual practice and psychological commitment and the claims of a Person who purports to express the intentions of an almighty God are really *intrusive*.

All this suggests that a teacher or parent interested in children's religious growth has to use every avenue through their youngsters' understandable defenses, even if it means brushing up on how children understand and accept objective facts— even unpleasant ones.

There are two hazardous extremes in the use of the human skills of reasoning: at one end, the tyranny of logic, demanding certitude before commitment; and at the other, abdication of logic, the blind leap, let 'er rip, and damn the torpedoes! I've tried to make the case that the core reason for sixteen years of formal education is to train young people to pilot a *balanced* course between those two extremes.

W. H. Auden wrote,

The sense of danger must not disappear:
The way is certainly both short and steep,
However gradual it looks from here;
Look if you like, but you will have to leap.

In *Fiddler on the Roof*, Tevye's religious traditions are the inflexible defense of his Jewish identity against the corruptions of the pagan outside world, but when his daughter defies that defense and marries a Christian, Tevye must hold himself from embracing her or even speaking to her, even when they are parting forever. At the other extreme, you have *Bonnie and Clyde*, *Boardwalk Empire*, and *Jersey Shore*.

Formal education has been, almost without exception, left brain, rational, utilitarian, and efficient. Even love poetry is used only as fodder for analysis. In fifty years, I never had a student who could explain any other reason why they were forced to read so much fiction. If there were a budget crunch, which would be cut: physics or music, math or art? It's as if the principles of the combustion engine and adding budget figures have more "value" in life than understanding and forgiveness.

A salutary way to counteract that prejudice toward the practical is to discuss the validity of the SATs as an even partial determinant of college suitability. It's a strictly left-brain assessment of a candidate's left-brain capabilities and attainments. The too-strict thinker would use the score almost exclusively to screen freshmen—something to which no student I have known would subscribe, and yet none would ever accept first-come-first-serve, with no qualifications whatever. In this personally relevant case, every student can readily see the impossibility of certitude and the need for latitude and risk taking, accepting less-than-compelling evidence like transcripts, student essays, and teacher recommendations.

It would be good for them to learn early that such a basis for decisions is almost always the *best* they're *ever* going to get for their *entire* lives: *probability*.

This balanced attitude toward apprehending, understanding, and evaluating reality sits uncomfortably with most Western minds—the rationally trained intelligence that would close down the Boonyville factory without a second thought for any values other than efficiency and profit.

The *Tao* (DAH-o) is a Confucian system of guidance. Like the Western idea of conscience or "philosophy of life" or moral principles, it is a way of evaluating all objects of our lives beyond the here-and-now utilitarian perspective. Although the titles are pronounced exactly the same, there is little likelihood that the Dow-Jones industrial averages would have much truck with the Confucian Tao. However, the Tao is no more or less alien to unrestricted monopoly capitalism than the principles of Jesus of Nazareth. There is little likelihood also that Dow companies would bedeck their office walls with needlepoint samplers of the Beatitudes.

There is no doubt that a parent's or teacher's comfortable understanding of the Tao would help a teenager expand his or her understanding and evaluation of life beyond the almost exclusively rational approach taught in almost all schools. The entire *Tao Te Ching* is available on the Internet, but it would almost surely be too daunting to start with. The *Britannica* is too fulsome, and even the scaled-down Wikipedia might be too tangled. However, the *BBC-Religions-Taoism* has a simple one-page summary for starters.

The importance of this consideration of the bipartisan brain and the need to access evidence with both analytical and intuitive understandings is essential to understanding the nature of faith, which is *both* discriminating *and* evaluating. However, on the way, it's a fusion of contrary skills that will be important in every decision your children will ever make, and as far as I know, it's rarely or ever explicitly taught in schools at secondary, collegiate, or graduate levels.

FOR REFLECTION

Consider the spectrum of approaches to the truth that the chapter explains, from "Give me absolute proof or forget it" at one end to "Full speed ahead and damn the torpedoes" on the other. One extreme demands almost total assurance before yielding, the other flies off in any direction on the whim of the moment. Which extreme do you lean more closely toward in making decisions in the following important areas: (1) entrusting an embarrassing problem to a friend, (2) commitment to your work, (3) sexual involvement, (4) relationship with God?

12

FAITH: A CALCULATED RISK

You don't have to see the whole staircase, just take the first step.
                                        —*Martin Luther King Jr.*

The question of faith is almost always the most effective segment of my course, not simply because it draws on the students' experience of trusting people in order to enlighten their understanding of how God "proves" himself, but because a teacher finally took time to talk to them about something genuinely *important* to *them* for a change.

When I occasionally ask high school and college kids whether they can tell me something that they and their peers consider really sacred, holy, or untouchable, they look blank. The very concept of holiness seems completely foreign. However, from my long experience with working with them, I can usually nudge them (at least most) to say "my family." Furthermore, I haven't the slightest doubt that only the sad outsiders would hesitate to say "my friends." The reflection question asking for a personal experience of stranger-to-best-friend progression is usually the longest and the most clearly heartfelt.

My comment on that reflection, almost always, is "Charlie, did you ever give *God* exactly this same chance to 'prove' himself?" It is, after all, the very reason I posed the question! So *that* I could write that comment.

As for the practical result—the openness of your child to a person-to-Person "connection to God" (religion), you and I have to content ourselves to be matchmakers. The best we can do is to bring the two principals together in as congenial way as possible. If the spark doesn't ignite, we can only go back to praying for it.

At the very least, this segment brings what faith means and what faith costs down-to-earth. Getting ambushed on the road to Damascus like St. Paul or getting jazzed by the Holy Spirit at an evangelical tent meeting is as rare as snow in the Congo. To expect to sit grumpily at Mass and get assaulted by God is as unreasonable as expecting to fall helplessly in love on a blind date. Hearken back to my squiring Catherine to her prom.

Faith, then—belief in our friends (perhaps including God)—is not an intellectual assent to a series of debatable propositions. It's a commitment of one's self; a gamble, a calculated risk.

In the introduction, I mentioned the contrary approach to religious education: top down, from revealed and demonstrated doctrine, acting as if those to be converted already had been. This opposite approach is based on long experience that led to the conclusion that almost no one in history has ever been awakened to religion—to a personal connection to God—as the result of an argument or a religion course or even 20 years of one course after the other. Any biography of conversion shows that conversions worth considering came from a *heart-to-heart* engagement between the God and God's "intended prey."

Like Augustine's *Confessions*: "Belatedly I loved thee, O Beauty so ancient and so new, belatedly I loved thee. For see, thou wast within and I was without, and I sought thee out there." Or Thérèse of Lisieux's *Story of a Soul*: "When one loves, one does not calculate."

Then there is God to Catherine of Siena: "Your capacity for sin can never exhaust my mercy," and in more recent times *The Seven-Storey Mountain* of Thomas Merton: "Souls are like athletes, that need opponents worthy of them, if they are to be tried and extended and pushed to the full use of their powers, and rewarded according to their capacity." Or C. S. Lewis's *Surprised by Joy*: "The hardness of God is kinder than the softness of men, and His compulsion is our liberation," and Anne Lamott's *Traveling Mercies*: "I thought such awful thoughts that I cannot even say them out loud because they would make Jesus want to drink gin straight out of the cat dish."

Of course, these quotations are nothing new. Read the Hebrew Scriptures of Abraham dancing a fugue with Yahweh trying to tease down the number slain in Sodom; Jacob *wrestling* with God; Moses trying to weasel out of his challenge; Jonah trying to outfox God by shipping out on a vessel headed for Tarshish on the far side of Spain; and Jeremiah cursing the day he was born to be God's prophet.

Every stage in moving from being an "Anonymous" to becoming a "Best" friend is an act of faith.* If you notice a stranger and only say, "Hello," you risk them becoming a leech or a bore. If you give them some time and talk, the risk gets more intense. They're *bound* to surprise you, for ill but also for good, and the closer they get to that hypersensitive innermost circle, the more dangerous the relationship becomes. This is why sex makes a relationship super-fragile.

A point to keep making is that faith is not just some special obscure relationship restricted to God and religion—which only saints and experts *really* fathom. It's an aspect of all human relationships, that's called into play all day, every day. Every time students take a note in class, it's an act of trust that the teacher knows what he or she is talking about. No one saw the Big Bang or a live dinosaur or a Neanderthal or an atom. We have only effects that we're sure are true, and then we string together evidence with logical connectors and arrows that end up pointing mostly toward a single least inadequate answer. Experts with a lot of know-how make *educated guesses* that fill in the *empty* spaces between the very little specific evidence we have and offer us *trustworthy opinions* about the (so far) likeliest explanation. (If only high school science teachers would be that less-than-certain, as expert scientists are.) However, almost nothing we claim to "know" is based either on wild conjecture or on never-to-be-challenged certainties.

The same is true when you accept doctors' diagnoses about body parts they can't directly see yet and submit in faith to their

---

*Cf. William O'Malley, *Meeting the Living God*, 4th ed. (Mahwah, NJ: Paulist Press, 2014), 203.

cutting us open—and you have no access to their medical school transcripts, nor could you interpret them expertly if you did. When you buy a used car, it's good to have a friend who knows something about engines to go with you. Finally, if you're not a sack of nerves on your wedding morning, there's something wrong with you.

Over the years, the students I've taught tend to close up when I have asked them to write what they thought their parents felt about their own friendship with God. More and more, they would say, "We don't talk about that kinda stuff at home." I began to believe that most parents have been leaving the faith lives of their children exclusively to me, and perhaps Sunday worship, which for the most part turned off even the parents. For some unfocused reason, parents think that it's "important" to start kids going to "church" early (like toilet training), even though it's counterproductively incomprehensible, and then— even to threats of no car on the weekend—to keep them grinding away at it through adolescence. The puzzlement is that, if this "religion business" is so "important," very few parents (clearly *excluding* the present readers) think it important enough to ready themselves to accompany their kids on the journey to Bethlehem, Capernaum, and Calvary.

Okay. It's important! So how do I communicate that as a parent or teacher?

Again, if you insisted on reading your children to sleep every night, and bought them books instead of *Resident Evil* or *Grand Theft Auto* games, they're likely to fare far better on the SATs. Similarly, if you taught them centering prayer as little kids and took them for nature walks and told them to listen for God's whispering, enriching their friendship with God now will be easier. However, judging from students' reflections, my hunch is that, if you were to say, "Let's talk about God," they'd react the same way they'd react if you said, "I saw Elvis in the CVS today."

That's expectable. The first disciples reacted the same way when Jesus returned to them after his crucifixion.

Keep remembering Annie Sullivan and Helen Keller: slow and persistent; drawing clues in their (as yet) uncomprehending hands. You could learn a lesson, too, from doing the opposite of what the Buddha's royal father did: shielding him from any distasteful sights in order to defend him from any upsetting, unanswerable questions, like why people are poor, get sick and old, and die. Every philosopher from Buddha to Karl Marx started with suffering in their quest for the reasons to keep trying, and every coming-of-age story since the Caves of Altamira was propelled by an endless succession of conflicts.

If you see a derelict on the street, instead of distracting your kids, why not ask, "Nobody would *choose* that way to live, would they? What do you think happened to that man to bring him from when he was just like you to that sad place?" When they get a bit older, ask them to go with you on a midnight run, or maybe one Saturday a month give up watching the game and help out in a soup kitchen. That's not God, but it's the people in whom we find Jesus.

Grace at meals takes no time; just remembering to do it. After all, heartfelt gratitude is what *Eucharist* means. However, here's a tiny warning: be sure to insist that "having enough" is nothing to be ashamed of, and that acknowledging giftedness is a reminder of how lucky we've been. In the stories of the Arthurian knights, good fortune—food, clothing, mansions—was wrongly attributed to the good luck of having highborn parents, but the best of them saw that *noblesse oblige*, privilege has an in-built price, in other words, to be treated as a noble, one is obliged to *act* nobly. In my college ethics class, I ask the students to fire off adjectives that are compacted into the word *noble*.

We will never lack for "God moments"—9/11, Iraq, the Boston Marathon Massacre—that provoke the question "How could a good God—?"

FOR REFLECTION

Several parents have told me that they spend the ride home from Mass shredding the celebrant's homily. A more imaginative parent might ask, "How much do you think God is stymied by a lackluster performance?" Or "How much of the lack of enthusiasm comes from *our* side?"

Consider also the process described in the chapter of moving from noticing, to sharing time and talk, to sacrificing together, to self-disclosure. Describe a situation in your own life when you yourself have gone through this same process by which a total stranger gradually became a best friend. As a parent or teacher, you may share with your youngsters the very first time you noticed your spouse. What intrigued you to pursue that person and what specific moment pushed you to say, "Yes. You're the one"?

II

DOES GOD EXIST?

13

DEATH:
THE CRUCIAL MYSTERY

If Cinderella says, "How is it that I must leave the ball at twelve?" her godmother might answer, "How is it that you are going there till twelve?"
—G. K. Chesterton

Often the most off-putting moment for parents with an adolescent is the talk about the "facts of life." Some find it too embarrassing. "We've never talked openly about this." What is worse is the fear "What if he or she knows far more about this than I suspect?" A more thoughtful response would be "How do I keep the subject *both* down-to-earth *and* sacred, special?" However, beneath the hesitation, if we want credibility and healthy, life-ready kids, we have to help them realize that, just as with sex, it's okay—in fact, essential—to talk about death. It's far better to open the subject rather than risk them having misconceptions about death, as even many adults at least pretend to, such as "It's so far away that it's as good as unreal....Grandpa's just on a vacation and will be back soon—like cartoon characters who get blasted and pop back up again....Only old people die." It's just possible that some youngsters might take wild risks to "prove" that they do have control over their own mortality.

Death isn't a topic that parents like to discuss, and because a youngster's personal experiences with natural deaths are less frequent than ever before in history, there are fewer counterweights to media's continual, contrived, and often ghastly but remote deaths. Kids see at least one death every day in the media and every minute or two in carnage videogames, not to mention now "the walking dead" and sexy androgynous vampires and werewolves.

Psychologists find that many younger children can't distinguish between fantasy and reality, making them more open to misunderstanding death. Surely, by the time they reach adolescence, death needs talking about.

Sooner rather than later, we owe it to our youngsters to face "with serenity the things that can't be changed." They have to accept, as the chapter tries to present, that death is inevitable, unpredictable, and irreversible. Otherwise, we arm them for reality with a comforting illusion.

Teenagers, fresh into their ability to rationalize and criticize, are already questioning the "imposed wisdom" of adults, including the moral matrix and "Good God" theology. "What good is it to give your guts to someone you love when they're only gonna get ripped out? It just isn't *fair* when somebody dies before they've had a real chance to live....If you really believe that 'he's happier in heaven now with Grandma again,' then why are you crying?"

However, I'll wager that very few parents believe death is as important to confront as sex is. In fact, I'll bet that dilemma never even arises. "We simply won't burden them with that." If that's true, then give up hope that Christianity can be meaningful because Christianity is all about death—and resurrection.

A truth to remember is that it's easier to talk about complex truths like death *objectively*, at a distance, long *before* we get into the emotional turmoil of explaining death when it waylays the kids unexpectedly in real life. Every time I've helped celebrate a teenager's funeral Mass, the churches were packed to the walls, and the incomprehension was *palpable*.

Death writes *finis* to everything that's preceded it (at least here). "Pens down! That's all she wrote." Death gives the *ultimate* perspective to life and demonstrates the relative values of everything. Which is objectively more important now: having the integrity that refuses to cheat or my dad becoming angry at an F grade; a quick sexual satisfaction or the sacredness of the person I'm with; an afternoon out with my friends or the family visit to Grandma in the nursing home? Perspective.

We'd all like kids to take a quantum leap beyond "crime and punishment" as a motive for decent, adult behavior. Making death real is an opportunity to bring that about: to see and *feel* the difference between the "heft" of being cut from a team or missing out on a lead in the play versus missing out on life itself? Furthermore, why is it more life giving to take hold of your own disappointment and bruised ego than quickly finding something else to fill the hurtful empty space, to stick your chin out and start over? Paradoxically, death opens up life! After all, isn't that what a great deal of their futures will require: death and starting over?

The subject needs more confident balance than a tightrope walker. Every youngster, even in the same family, is a unique individual. Some can't abide pussyfooting; some loathe confrontation. To create an overawareness of death can be crippling, with kids reading every label on every can and becoming afraid to cross the street. Yet to leave them blasé about death is equally disabling, denying them the enriching human attitudes that ownership of death allows: the awareness of how precious time is and how lucky we are to be here at all; how important it is to tell people we love them and how crippling it is to nurse grudges.

As in every important question, it's not only acceptable but laudable to say, "You got me there. I just don't know. Let me mull it over a bit, okay?" Even teachers can still learn.

Death is the chance to move kids' motivations from fear and hope of reward, and even beyond loyalty and dutifulness, into personal principles.

Probably *the* most potent argument against God—at least a provident, caring God—is the existence of unmerited suffering. "How could a good God allow...?" It simply can't be avoided. Failing to confront this question jeopardizes the whole enterprise. Some overly confident young people can say quite brashly, "I've got the guts to face life without the crutch of belief in God." However, their bravado goes limp at the coffin of a parent, or at the funeral of a classmate suicide, or doing a service project with special needs children or incontinent old people. Shield them from those facts of life, and you shield them from God.

The only honest response is "It's God...or nothing." There is no other alternative.

There is an iron-hard dichotomy: our existence is the result of choice or chance; no other possibility. *Either* some Mind, capable of seeing alternatives and choosing purposefully, caused everything, *or* everything that exists came about simply as a result of a string of lucky accidents. The saying "accidentally...on purpose" is a joke, meaning the perpetrator is pretending that his or her mistake was caused by Fate or sheer chance or by the devil, but it really was intentional. It can't be both. Choice and chance negate one another.

So here are the alternatives: a God with justifiable (if unreadable) reasons or haphazard accidents with *no* justification. At least believers in God have someone to *blame*. If there's no God, then no one has a reason, and no one's to blame. If you get rid of God, you also have to get rid of any "justification" for misborn children, sickness, aging, and death itself, as well as hurricanes, droughts, and tsunamis. Then there's also the fact that mindless evolution stumbled one blind, "cruel" step too far and came up with a species like us that can be *willfully* cruel, that can invent torments like carpet bombing, anthrax, and poison gas that no other creature could do. Moreover, this accidental species is the only one that knows that death will wipe out everything they've ever tried to do, and that there is absolutely *no* reason or purpose to it.

The brilliant microbiologist Richard Dawkins sums up more honestly what genuine atheists realize they must forfeit if they dismiss God: "This is one of the hardest lessons for humans to learn. We cannot admit that things might be neither good nor evil, neither cruel nor kind, but simply callous—indifferent to all suffering, lacking all purpose."* And more fully:

> We humans have purpose on the brain. We find it hard to look at anything without wondering what it is 'for,' what the motive for it is, or the purpose behind it. When the obsession with purpose becomes pathological it is called paranoia—reading malevolent

---

*Richard Dawkins, *A River Out of Eden* (New York: Basic Books, 1995), 95f.

purpose into what is actually random bad luck. But this is just an exaggerated form of a nearly universal delusion.*

Because Dawkins refuses the idea of "purpose"—independently of an individual's ideas—he needn't feel hampered by the need to figure out *why* this demand for purpose is "nearly universal" in humans, which he admits is true. There is no need to ask why our species—*alone*—is cursed with a hunger for a food —purpose, meaning, justice, answers, a reason to keep going— that doesn't exist.

If Dawkins is right, then in a godless universe we have to fabricate and choose our own purpose—our own self-justified reason to keep going—even when life is hell for a long time.

It's objectively baseless; a delusion, but it does give us a lifeline to cling to in the storms. No delusion is better than any other. If your "Grand Illusion" is to cure cancer, or the Guinness record for most toothpick Eiffel Towers, or ridding the European continent of Jews and Slavs, so be it.

Well then, why not delude oneself that there is a God, who does have a purpose, which is evident from the way we're made? At the end of your rope, it's as good an argument as any.

Of course, Christianity rests squarely on the resurrection of Jesus. In 1 Corinthians 15:14, St. Paul said that if Jesus didn't rise from death, *all* that Christianity claims is cut to nothing. Empty. However, resurrection itself is one more vacuous notion if death isn't an accepted reality. Once again, we're caught selling space heaters to Eskimos and kitty litter to Bedouins.

Each year, I give quick questionnaires to my high school and college theology classes before I treat Christianity, just to be sure that I'm not belaboring them with stuff they already know and accept. The results are, just as the mammoth young peoples' survey, *Soul Searching*, mentioned earlier, also testifies: "moralistic therapeutic deism," placebo Christianity, Hallmark spirituality, and Jesus the Warm Fuzzy.

In the survey, I ask, "What did Jesus save us *from*?" and they keep answering, "From sin." Why? That's what they were

---

*Ibid., 96.

told, just like the sum of two plus two or the atomic number of hydrogen; and most often less consequential.

However, if Jesus "saved us from sin," why didn't he save me from *sinning*? Pretty ineffective for an alleged omnipotent God! In fact, from the start, why didn't this all-seeing God make us like every other creature: capable of doing only what will make us contented?

No, Jesus came to save us from *fear*—fear that our sins might be unforgivable and fear that death might be the negation of everything for each of us, but, of course, neither of those *are* genuine fears for our young audience, if guilt trips are bad for you and death is less real than the Yellow Brick Road to Emerald City.

Youngsters need to face death, not only in order to face life but to face religion.

FOR REFLECTION

Your true attitudes and values appear not in what you say but in the day-to-day ways you act. Consider the real, concrete, specific ways you respond to work, challenges, other people, especially your family. Does a real acceptance of your eventual death (next week, next year) suggest ways in which you ought to change your handling of work, challenges, and other people? This question may be a dead giveaway about how seriously you take the most basic facts of life.

14

ATHEISM

*If the whole universe has no meaning, we should never
have found out that it has no meaning.*

—C. S. Lewis

Any salesperson who refuses to acknowledge the attractiveness
of the competition (all that multifaceted, enticing pagan propaganda) is doomed. The strongest opposition to "The God
Option" is out-and-out atheism. (The most common and effective is indifference.) To project the untruth that our answer to
the question of human purpose is the *only* sensible one, as many
dedicated Catholics do, is at the very least naïve and at worst
completely dishonest and repugnant. Many people get along
just fine without God, and youngsters, especially the smartest,
are keenly aware of that. Catholics have to be aware that we no
longer live in Christendom, but rather in the culture of
Narcissism.* Those afflicted with Catholic certitude never confront Camus's honest, down-to-earth assertion that the core of
the human quest is "to find a reason for living."

Don't offer them Jesus till you've hooked their attention
with that question of human value; the most effective way of
posing the question is "What gives you the *right* to feel good
about yourself?" Furthermore, don't expect to divert their attention from more pressing enjoyments if you yourself have already
convinced them that "the reason for living" is making a living
and the financial security to satisfy their desires. If the only
motive you can offer for spending sixteen years of effort—and
your money—enslaved to the school system is so that they can
make even more money, then be honest and simply set aside

---

*See the book of that title, *The Culture of Narcissism*, by Christopher Lasch.

religion, which is talking about a totally *other* Reality where numbers are useless. The two are as different as justice and mercy. One goes much, much further than the other.

That's the reason we began with what validates opinions and then asked the comprehensive exam question the Son of Man will ask at the Final Judgment: "What does 'success' mean to you as an individual?" Every other expression of *anything's* value lines up before that question like metal filings before a magnet or Hitler Youth at a Nuremberg rally.

We all want "Success." No matter how you de-compact and specify the idea, it means that you find some way to make your life *matter*, or at the very least *not be negligible*.

Atheists claim that belief in a validating God is wishful thinking. Believers could lob that grenade right back by claiming that denying a God who has a willed purpose for us is just an "if only."

In my experience, what many adolescents, newly invested in the ability to reason, are doing when they claim atheism has almost nothing to do with God. It's asserting not a belief but merely asserting independence. It's as shallow a statement as a tattoo. What makes it even more pseudo is that they so blithely ignore what's wrapped up in their denial. Not only do they deny merely the trespass of an omnipotent God on their freedom, as well as the intrusion of an out-of-it clerical class, thought-police, which many stalwart believers also do in actual practice. They implicitly deny *ipso facto* what every *thinking* atheist takes for granted: our ingrained human urge to find reasons is a curse.

They've never heard that the greatest argument *for* a purposeful God is how godforsaken life is *without* God. They can't seem to encompass the inescapable atheist corollary that every genuine sense of "success" or "purpose" or "fulfillment" we find is ultimately a cruel self-delusion. It's all Monopoly money, and so are we, once we get put back into the box.

Now that we find that hell is no longer in session to scare kids to virtue and worship, the outcome is even bleaker. There is not even the intriguing sadism of Dante's *Inferno*—just annihilation. I can't recall a single "atheist" teenager in fifty years who accepted *that* corollary. When I pose it, there is the confident claim, "I can take that!" However, they tend to back down a few steps when I say, "Can you see yourself saying that at your mother's coffin? 'She's just a piece of dirt from now on'"?

Another rock-bottom, and cogent, objection to God: both God and atoms are invisible. You can set up experiments to validate the presence—and power—of atoms, but not to prove the presence of God. This statement is only partially true. That syllogism restricts the word to *laboratory* experiments, which is reductionist. Dating and an engagement are experiments. Can anyone set up a lab experiment to demonstrate the presence and intensity of love? Just as a scientific polygraph reveals not truth but merely the client's pulse and sweat, by trying to validate claims of love, strict science can reveal only increased heartbeats, heavy breathing, and so forth, and argue *from* that data *to* conclusions that are more-or-less probable. The difficulty comes from most teenagers' unfounded belief that experimental scientists are far more certain than the scientists themselves dare to claim.

There are two ways to get *probable* validation of the existence and presence of God. The first uses the same deductive processes that scientists and detectives use: eliminating inadequate answers and narrowing the possibilities. The second way of allowing God to "prove" himself is exactly the same process by which any other person proves him- or herself: noticing, time and talk, opening the self to the other—the same process by which Helen Keller discovered that she wasn't alone. No one knows a friend via a textbook or a succession of rational arguments. The experiment is called praying—not saying prayers, but opening one's inner self to the Friend.

One can say, "I tried that once, but it didn't work." Once again, this is naïve ignorance of genuine experimental science. No researcher goes into the lab seeking the cure for cancer and expects to find it on the first try. The researcher is only looking for *promising new evidence.*

Another objection is "No one *needs* God." That's iron evidence of the speaker's confident inexperience. (Less tolerant and loving teachers call it "arrogant ignorance" and give up.) The usual counterarguments are to put the objector in a foxhole with tracer bullets zipping a foot overhead; put him or her next to the coffin of a teenage suicide; sit down with a mother whose child just died in the ER after being caught in the crossfire. Furthermore, have her or him visit a facility where loving but helpless parents have put their impaired children. Now, do you think you need a reason to make sense of this situation? Do you still honestly believe there's no need for *somebody* who has a legitimate motive for allowing this to occur? Or are you prepared, in your gut, and not your head, to say, "Oh well! That's the breaks. Dumb luck! Keep a stiff upper lip, okay?"

Most kids I've taught haven't been hurt enough to be true atheists.

There is another cluster of God-objections that flock around apparent contradictions that are built right into the definition of God. For example, if God has foreknowledge, why doesn't he prevent bad things? Or if God's omnipotent, why doesn't he step in and rectify the whole mess? On that same line of argument, if he's so smart, why have 99 percent of his creations died out, huh?

Such protests give rise to yet another dumb objection that God is just a crutch that humans made up to scare away their fear of death. If this is the case, why didn't we make up a God at least as smart as we are, more accommodating, tractable, and "nicer"?

In turn, the objection exposes what might be *the* biggest obstacle to God: even allowing the possibility of God inescapably calls into question *my own* importance. Have you ever met an adolescent whose personal shortcomings and setbacks didn't appear to them more monumental than the woes of Job? If there is Somebody who does—impossibly—fill all the requirements for an entity to be "God," my desires, goals, and agendas have to yield in importance to his/hers/theirs. Sorry! That's intolerable. Then honesty dies, and with it, the Quest.

Another objection is the unfounded antagonism between God and science. Listening to well-meaning science teachers, even in Catholic schools, youngsters come away with the notion that "God" is just a label misapplied to the combined forces of cosmology, evolution, and the laws of physics. If that assertion were true, it would invalidate the existence of any entity outside our minds who verifies our ideas of God. There is no need to get down on your knees and thank a mindless "Force" or expect any interpersonal relationship. There's no person there. Gravity and evolution merely stumble forward. Why? The question displays your gullibility.

Finally, there is an unfounded objection generated by well-meaning teachers—even among our most dedicated religious education teachers. It goes without saying that volunteer teachers of religion after school or on Sundays have never had any serious preparation beyond a few college courses, which seemed hardly important at the time, and perhaps a few necessarily brief summer courses. There's a reason why the saying "A little knowledge is a dangerous thing" became a cliché. This is true especially in regard to the truth that Scripture—in both testaments—is definitely not the result of videotapes and eyewitness reporting. A great deal of it is not—as all the catechism writers seem to believe—to impart *information* but to effect *conversion*. The writers are more interested in interpretation than in information.

Such partially prepared—and generous—teachers hear in workshops that the Scripture is a fabric of "myths." They then pass that along, without realizing that their audiences, and perhaps even they themselves, are mishearing the word. In ordinary parlance, glossy magazines, and even national news programs, the word *myth* denotes a widely held but *false* belief, as in "Vietnam destroyed the myth that America could never lose a war." The more sophisticated understanding is a story or theory that attempts to capture a truth of human life, as in the myth of Pandora to "explain" proliferation of evil, or *Jack and the Beanstalk* carrying the truth that, if you want to be a rich man, you have to contend with "giants." Atomic science is an attempt to give physical grounding to realities that are untouchable. In that sense, the story of Adam and Eve never literally happened, but it tells an unarguable truth: put two human beings in a perfect place and they *will* crap it up. That never happened as written, yet it happens every day. *The Catcher in the Rye* never happened historically, but it tells more truth about male adolescent psychology than any psychology book. The Genesis snake never talked, but "his" voice still comes out of every TV on the planet. Most people today are no more aware of his wiles than those first two befuddled nudists.

Scripture requires a mind more concerned with "meaningful" than with "accurate."

FOR REFLECTION

You can't choose with true freedom unless you've honestly considered all the real alternatives. Even if you do strongly believe in God—or if you're rather convinced there is no God—what are your honest reactions to the three major areas in this chapter of the student text: (1) the atheists' reasons for believing in the lack of probability of a Mind-Behind-It-All, (2) the view of human life they are logically forced to accept, and (3) the substitutes they accept for a purposeful life?

15

THE GREAT HUNGER: THE SOUL

For what is a man profited, if he shall gain the whole world and lose his own soul? Or what shall a man give in exchange for his soul?

—*Matthew 16:26*

Since the Second Vatican Council, it is hard to find a Catholic who would dare to speak out loud about "losing your soul." Yet the same teachers who avoid that unnerving concept give classes on the Holocaust and fail to ask the crucial question, "What did the people who conducted those camps lack?" Some English teachers who teach Kafka's *Metamorphosis* blithely assert that "Society" took away Gregor Samsa's "human dignity," failing to suggest that Gregor also gave it up; that no one degrades you without your cooperation, nor do they ask where are the offices of this imperious, unchallengeable Society? No one says that commercials and reality TV shows are leaching out our children's invitation to become adult human beings—their souls. After an evening of *Survivor, Transformers, Jersey Shore,* and *The Bachelorette* (or whatever shows inevitably take their places), you may want to ask how far we've come from the days of the Coliseum.

More recently, the distinguished microbiologist Richard Dawkins, one of the world's brightest, most articulate scientists, declared that losing your soul, your self, your meaning, and purpose is not really that big a deal. Your soul is your self. So you're no big deal either, despite your delusions:

> This is one of the hardest lessons for humans to learn. We cannot admit things might be neither good nor

evil. Neither cruel nor kind, but simply callous—indifferent to all suffering, lacking all purpose....We humans have purpose on the brain. We find it hard to look at anything without wondering what it is "for," what the motive for it is, or the purpose behind it. When the obsession with purpose becomes pathological it is called paranoia—reading malevolent purpose into what is actually random bad luck. But this is just an exaggerated form of a nearly universal delusion.*

Dr. Dawkins dismisses the core of humanity as merely bothersome, like an appendix—even though he himself admits that this "delusion" is almost without exception in all humans.

Those first two paragraphs sound like an ironclad fundamentalist preacher in a revival tent, no? Like the flare-eyed berobed quacks in *The New Yorker* cartoons with "Doom!" signs...that's exactly my intention. Prophets are always unwelcome at orgies—exaggerated, to be sure, but pointed in the right direction.

More and more often, in both high school and college students, something vital seems to be missing. They don't *seem* to have any awareness of the other-worldly, the transcendent. The extent of the background against which they judge meaningful values is circumscribed by a strictly "this-world" life, and even that life is unrealistically open-ended, since death is as close to unreal now as cavities and failure.

The following story pulls kids up short in puzzlement:

One day an African boy, wandering in the forest, suddenly stopped, spellbound by birdsong trilling somewhere overhead. The melody soared and swooped and cascaded, as if the soul of the bird were winging from her throat. And then there she was, perched on a branch above his head, resplendent in feathers of blood red and iridescent blue. She cocked a quizzical eye at him and fluttered down to his bare shoulder, grasping it gently in her silver talons.

---

*Richard Dawkins, *River Out of Eden* (Basic Books: New York, 1996), 112.

Gleefully the boy ran home with his prize, bursting into the hut just as his father returned, grim and empty-handed from the hunt. "Father," the boy cried, "look what I found! Isn't she beautiful? What shall we feed her?"

"Feed her?" his father growled. "What shall we feed your brothers and sisters? There is nothing!" The father grasped the bird from the boy's shoulder and strangled its cries. "Now," he said darkly, "we can live one more day."

But in killing the bird, he had killed the song. And in killing the song, he had killed himself.

In reading this story, students suspect they are missing something crucial themselves, which is precisely the reaction I'm hoping for. Deep down somewhere (in their souls), they know that their meaning is more substantial than their sneakers, or their complexions, or their GPAs. For most, it's the first time anybody brought that elusive entity to their attention. However, something that preexisted the Electronic Age in all humans knows that there's *something* about them that demands respect.

The terms *soul* and *spirit* have been bastardized in "soul food" and "soul music," even Kia "soul cars," which are to the real thing what bubble gum is to nourishment. The words are as valueless and meaningless as penny coins.

Arthur Miller exposes the soulless vacuum in *Death of a Salesman*, Paddy Chavesky in *Network*, Tennessee Williams and Edward Albee in just about everything they wrote. However, it's present, too, in the evening soporifics for anyone sensitive enough to discern the soullessness. And yet again, it *seems* that our young have adapted with shells of protective Teflon, tolerance for mayhem and evil—like video games and slaughter movies. Without realizing, humanity was dribbling away through the cracks in the society we've settled for. Headlines about infants in Dumpsters, wars across the world that settle nothing, school massacres, political malfeasance—they're all as ignorable as shrieking sirens and arrogant graffiti, and nobody seems able—or willing, or even interested—in doing anything to change that situation—except you and me.

Like the Adam and Eve story, and so many others, Genesis 25 shows us this human penchant for bartering one's soul for cheap goods:

> Once when Jacob was cooking a stew, Esau came in from the field, and he was famished. Esau said to Jacob, "Let me eat some of that red stuff, for I am famished!"...Jacob said, "First sell me your birthright." Esau said, "I am about to die; of what use is a birthright to me?" Jacob said, "Swear to me first." So he swore to him, and sold his birthright to Jacob. Then Jacob gave Esau bread and lentil stew, and he ate and drank, and rose and went his way. Thus Esau despised his birthright. (Gen 25:29–34)

Comment is hardly necessary. It almost surely never happened, but it's true.

The most profound evidence of a Reality beyond this reality is the universal human hunger that says, "This *can't* be all of it!" It's what I understand Richard Rohr, OFM, to mean when he speaks of the "homesickness." What southern slaves meant when they sang, "Sometimes I feels like a motherless child—a long wa-ay from home." We're the only species we know that is gut-insatiable. There is absolutely nothing in this present reality that satisfies for long enough. "I can't get no satisfaction....Is that all there *is*?...Tomorrow and tomorrow and tomorrow....There is no America. There is IBM and ITT and ATT and DuPont, Dow, and Exxon....What got lost?"

Without a purposeful God, those questions are absurd, and our hunger is a curse. Forget death. How do our kids face *life* without possession of their own souls?

FOR REFLECTION

When things get out of hand, at times when life at least seems unbearable, what do *you* cling to? What keeps you going? Where do you turn when nothing makes sense? No need to reveal anything you don't wish to.

16

THEISM

I would rather live my life as if there is a God and die to find out there isn't, than live as if there isn't and to die to find out that there is.

—*Albert Camus*

The key hidden underneath that quote is that if there isn't in fact a God, we'll never find out we were wrong. The challenge for teachers and parents is getting young people to find the God Questions personally significant and worth honest probing.

A truly real obstacle is unreal expectations—most of them formed by ostensibly innocent sources. First, the *Catechism* (50), based on a Vatican I decree given under pain of excommunication (DS 3004), states, "By natural reason man can know God with *certainty*, on the basis of his works" (emphasis mine). The demand from our audience for compelling certainty is deeply rooted. When every other salesforce gives guarantees, the government makes them pay up. Well?

After experiencing the confidence of the voices of the official Church and reading the *Catechism* and watching biblical films, the baptized-but-unconverted somewhat understandably are waiting for a burning bush or at the very least a lightning flash on the road to Damascus. Neither they nor their preceptors seem to realize that such dramatic inducements would call for a world-class miracle for every single convert! The best anyone can get on the God Questions—or any other question, for that matter—is what Thomists call "*moral* certainty," that is, the same as-sure-as-possible conviction jurors have when they vote "without *reasonable* doubt." Confident, not compelled. Probability!

Faith and certitude are as incompatible as love and enslavement. Both Cardinal Newman and Søren Kierkegaard espoused a way of understanding that was neither the stainless-steel rational structure of an empirical disputation nor the intuitive leap some feel with "love at first sight." Rather, it's the much more commonplace, slow accumulation of evidence—converging probabilities—where what at first seemed random disconnected bits begin to turn into arrows, all, or at least most of them pointing toward the only viable answer. Read a detective novel, watch a courtroom drama, visit a pharmaceutical lab, ask a couple why they stayed married for fifty years, or take a lesson from Goldilocks!

Especially in a classroom setting, it's difficult to make young people realize that this *isn't* just one more boring academic puzzle, like "Are there other intelligent beings on other planets?" Most students I've known are more than willing to concede that, given the laws of probability, there "must be" such beings. Why? Precisely because it *is* just one more busywork mental labyrinth like "Find the cosine of angle AOC" or "What's the answer to the Riddle of the Sphinx?" Some math or science teacher or some episode of *Nova* claimed it, and, since it doesn't affect their personal choices the way their parents' religion does, why not? Science is dependable.

The God Questions are really the-Value-of-*You* questions. This is the time in adolescents' lives when their "new" bodies call them to a more substantial awareness of themselves and the world from which they've been shielded. It should also be the beginning of a completely new kind of commitment to themselves and to the world. If they can deal with *Hamlet* and macroeconomics, they ought to begin learning what will make them genuinely fulfilled. In order to do that in honesty, they must confront the ultimate dichotomy: Were they made with an intended purpose, or do they have to fumble around and come up with their own purpose—till death wipes them out?

Either way, teachers and parents are *obligated* by their roles to prepare the children in their charge to face adult life—not as we or they would *hope* it will be, but as it *is*.

In order to lock in their attention on that one, I interpose the subject of death. Dr. Samuel Johnson famously said, "Depend upon it, sir, when a man knows he is to be hanged in a fortnight, it concentrates his mind."* However, with all the distractions and all the trivialization and denial of death in their upbringing, the shocking insight of their own mortality in religion class will have dissipated by the time they get to gym class. That's why also facing the question at home shows that this isn't just "school stuff," or worse, just "religion stuff." Parents may no longer wrestle with quadratic equations or Napoleon, but they are genuinely concerned about motives for leading a decent life; a matter that is intimately affected by the reality of death.

Whether they are ready or not, in order to qualify to be treated as adults, teenagers have to seriously confront the truths that have concerned adults and eluded children since the rise of *Homo sapiens*.

The first challenge is the somewhat-too-simple response to the unreal antagonism between God and science offered by Creationism and by Intelligent Design—not that we should deny *either* one! We merely challenge their reductionism; their cramped view of God.

Creationism resents and resists any role that chance could play in cosmology or evolution—in effect short-changing or outright denying the staggering fertility of the original "stuff" called into being, and what's more, because they themselves are so all-fired serious and businesslike, denying God's playfulness! Creationists ignore the truth that, outside time, God has never aged and is therefore "younger" than any of us! They refuse to entertain the possibility that efficiency is clearly not as important to God as it is to those who try to explain God.

Intelligent Design rightly challenges exclusively materialist explanations that claim that everything we encounter today came into existence from a nearly infinite series of sheer accidents, that there is simply no need of a Designer, because everything was already there "in the mix." Followers of this viewpoint seem never to have found the need to ascertain just how that

_____

*James Boswell, *The Life of Samuel Johnson* (New York: Everyman's Library, 1993), 748.

ever-so-fortunate mixture and its governing laws just happened to stumble together out of nowhere.

Therefore, one more iron alternative: either an infinite, boundlessly fertile, uncaused and accidental material universe, or an infinite, boundlessly creative, uncaused and purposeful immaterial Deity. (Stephen Hawking ups the ante by postulating an infinite *series* of infinite universes.)

What makes both followers of Creationism and Intelligent Design rightly anxious is the exclusively materialists' use of the word *random*. When the smartest kids hear the word *random*, they hear "haphazard, helter-skelter, and *sheer* chance"—which are also what a rigid philosopher hears—and therefore inherently *purposeless*, which would immediately negate God. However, that is simply not what *serious* scientists mean. Early science teachers have never clarified what cautious professionals mean by *random*.

They do *not* mean "causeless, aimless, and indiscriminate." The very core of science is the law of cause and effect. Rather their meaning is *imperfectly predictable*. "Chance mutations" take place within *regulatory* (which requires intelligence) constructions in any particular situation. They are mutations, or departures from a *consistent norm* of behavior. Therefore, knowing those physical constants—those *laws*—experts can make educated guesses about each situation; very much in the manner of highly experienced Vegas odds makers.

Educated guesses = calculated risks = acts of confident *faith*. Like theologians, scientists can come to a *high degree of probability*.

For the past fifty years this is not what high school and college students come to understand. In fact, they haven't the slightest resistance to the belief that every single entity that exists today came about from a super-infinite number of very fortunate rolls of the dice. It's what they've been taught.

I've rarely, if ever, found a high school or college student, even one with *only* Catholic education, who found the slightest materialist explanation not only possible but undeniable. They have no hesitation whatever in accepting that, as Carl Sagan asserted, "One day, quite by accident, a molecule discovered a way to make crude copies of itself." If true, such a claim would accept the *possibility* of getting blood out of a brick, a scream from a cabbage, and the words "To be or not to be" out of a rabbit. On the contrary, I have quite frequently had students question the law of cause and effect: "No effect can exceed the capabilities of its causes."

What is lacking in Intelligent Design is their assertion that, after the Big Bang, God had to keep stepping back in again to "adjust": personally "trigger" growth in inert matter, sensation in vegetables, and logic in lower animals. If God is so almighty smart, why couldn't he have "seeded" all those potentialities into that precosmic "mix" like time-release capsules? Even more exciting is the thought that if Christians can accept that God could infuse himself into an invisible ovum within Mary of Nazareth, why could that same God not have chosen to infuse his divine self (intelligence, plans, providence, continued creativity) into that infinitesimal Singularity from which scientists claim the whole universe "must have" exploded? There is no need to step in later to upgrade or implement Plan B. As a result, Gerard Manley Hopkins was *literally* correct: "The world is charged with the grandeur of God"! All those images of God—in nearly all religions—as fiery power are *true*! St. Ignatius was right: "We find God *in* all things"!

Keep stressing that evidence is essential for any opinion, including faith in God, but that evidence is not the same as proof. Unlike Creationism and Intelligent Design, insofar as I can understand them, and certainly unlike the *Catechism*, this text does not start from unquestionable dogmas but from unquestionable *facts*. Remember always, too, that the high school and college years are the time students are *supposed* to be questioning—everything. I frequently have college students challenging my assertion that humans have a greater inner dignity than other animals. If they can negate that *fact*, then human sex is no different from any other natural animal coupling. However, they simply have to yield when you ask, "If you could save only one from death, would it be the human baby or the kitten?

FOR REFLECTION

Take a little time on this one. Review the various reasons for believing there's a greater probability God exists than the objections in this chapter.* Poke holes in them if you want. Don't involve yourself with specific doctrines or claims of a particular religion. Just stick to what convinces you personally about the question of *some* Mind-Behind-It-All.

---

*Cf. also William O'Malley, *Meeting the Living God*, 4th ed. (Mahwah, NJ: Paulist Press, 2014), 253–74.

III

WHAT IS GOD LIKE?

17

THE GOD OF THE PHILOSOPHERS

To see a World in a Grain of Sand
And a Heaven in a Wild Flower,
Hold Infinity in the palm of your hand
And Eternity in an hour.

—*William Blake*

From the outset, in order to short-circuit any resistance rooted in antagonisms against organized religion, it has been essential to exclude any references to any group's or individual's subjectively conditioned beliefs about God based on special revelation, and to offer evidence that should not abuse the trust of any honest mind. The quarry has been only *some* undifferentiated Mind-Behind-It-All, who could account for the ordered predictability of the universe, the apparent progress of evolution, and the hungers found only in humans, which are curses if they exist without any possibility of their fulfillment. The most profound of these is the "homesickness," the longing for some paradise where everything makes sense—symbolized in almost all cultures' creation myths by a Promised Land, Eden, Bhaishajyaguru, Utopia, Valhalla, Shangri-la, Nirvana, Pulotu, Shamba-hala, Elysium, Happy Hunting Ground, Avalon, and Tír na nÓg.

The homesickness seems universally to be a constitutive part of being human. We all feel like *émigrés* from our true homeland. However, in recent years there seems to be less and less awareness or concern or importance in high school and college students of the sacred, the holy, and the transcendent: what

Bonhoeffer calls God—"the Beyond in our midst."* In fact, except for "my family" and "my friends," when we discuss our way through the fog of comforting abstractions and platitudes, few have a felt interest in anything nonmaterial. This is an unnerving insight, but you can check it out yourself. For example, would you ordinarily prefer a retreat or a rock concert? Will the core motive for your career choice be helping others or financial security? It's hard to imagine how many people, growing up in our pseudo-Christian, pagan society could be more than remotely altruistic. The fact that some truly are interested in the nonmaterial is indeed a miracle, but they are very, very few.

Our young can't help growing up cautious if they have even the slightest awareness from history or the daily papers how human beings can degrade themselves and one another: everybody cheats, everybody lies, and paranoia is no more than a realistic response to the status quo. Furthermore, it's no longer just reports from our local village; the message is multiplied and amplified all around the planet: the rich get rich, and the poor get poorer; there's a sucker born every minute; do the other guy before he does you, and don't make a move without a guarantee.

We're not teaching Pollyanna and *Candide*. Just because we've had one class or chapter "establishing" the probability of a Mind-Behind-It-All, don't think that's overturned nearly two decades of incessant inducements to materialism, narcissism, and skepticism.

Over the centuries, the human intelligence and will, flexing after ever greater conquests in every area of life, has found ways to slip out from beneath our dependence on a Divine Personage who will fill in the gaps in our needs for answers, for relief, for justification. We can go it alone! Every century, every year, every day, we're "outgrowing God." So are our kids!

Actually, it started when the snake allegedly offered Eve the first chance to free humanity from its uncomfortable ties of subservience, gratitude, and obedience to an "alleged" God. Later, Protagoras (ca. 480–411 BCE) dared to suggest that "man is the measure of all things." Here was the first trickle of academic

---

*Dietrich Bonhoeffer, *Letters and Papers from Prison*, rev. ed., ed. Eberhard Bethge (New York: Macmillan, 1967), 155.

skepticism, or to be less judgmental, independent thinking. Protagoras is more or less echoed exactly by what Carl Sagan wrote at the outset of *Cosmos* 2,300 years later: "The cosmos is all there is and all there ever was and all there ever will be." Two generations ago, the Beatles called it "I get by with a little help from my friends. I get high with a little help from my friends." Has anything gotten more promising for God since then? After all, if you've got a credit card and a cell phone, who needs God?

In the Renaissance, God and the immaterial ceased to be certain assumptions. The link between natural laws and the existence of God and the soul were far from certain. Empirical science shifted the center of gravity from intangible to experimentally verifiable, from witchcraft to medicine, from the ivory towers of philosophy and theology to the verifications of the laboratory. As knowledge grew, demons solidified into viruses and botulisms. During the seventeenth-century Enlightenment, intellectuals scorned the naïveté of the unlettered and over the centuries have had more influence on universities that train national leaders, future educators, governments, public school systems, news commentators, slick magazines, and the man and woman in the street than the Sermon on the Mount. American attempts to make Freud acceptable to the hard-nosed American public purposely mistranslated the master's word *soul* into *mind*, as breakable into hard-and-fast bins as in the post office or a butcher shop. However, more persuasive was the rise of capitalism, the consoling self-validation underwritten by stock portfolios and other material assurances of personal value.

Many wise folk would claim that what got lost was the soul of society—civilization. Joseph Campbell wrote, "It may very well be that the very high incidence of neuroticism among ourselves follows the decline among us of such effective spiritual aid."* Once again, Esau surrendered his birthright for a bowl of stew.

Those among us who refuse to be hypocrites have always been thinking—all the way back to Adam—"Who needs God?" It's the primordial temptation for clever beings.

*Joseph Campbell, *The Hero with a Thousand Faces* (Novato, CA: New World Library, 2008), 7.

GOD'S NATURE: TRANSCENDENCE

God is unconquerably "Other." If indeed there is a Mind-Behind-It-All, he/she/they. But never "It" is the nth degree of everything: omnipotent, omniscient, omni-everything—limitless. However, that, too, is one of the most deeply rooted obstacles: if God is "the Last Word," I am, *ipso facto*, not. For a teenager, just emerging from near-autistic narcissism, that is a difficult fact to accept. However, year by year, unexpected intrusions, challenges, and defeats will make that surrender to the truth less and less avoidable. God is God and is not answerable to us. Accept that, or implode in frustration trying to make the truth untrue. Don't let children turn twenty-one without that awareness.

Take them to a planetarium or plug in any of the Internet sources like NASA's "How Big Is the Universe." If there is no "dimension" to reality beyond that incomprehensibly huge space, there is no word tiny enough to describe the insignificance of each one of us, no matter how arrogantly we posture, like Lilliputians before Gulliver showed up—and Gulliver is death.

However, IF there is a Fifth Dimension, and IF the Master of that and all dimensions purposely chose me, knows my name, and intends my fulfillment, the only response is "WOW!" The alternative is annihilation. Choose your matrix! How large are you willing to allow Reality to be?

Until we get our students and our children to crack open their horizons—even a horizon as near-infinite as the cosmos—they're going to live smaller lives than they have to settle for. If we want to give our kids "every opportunity," this is the biggest one!

GOD'S NATURE: IMMANENCE

Here is where newfound sophistication can definitely sour what Jesus meant when he told Nicodemus that we have to go back and regain our childhood in order to find God. The show-me attitude ingrained in humans since Adam, through the

Greek skeptics, the Enlightenment, the Industrial Revolution, and the Electronic Global Village disdains susceptibility of the mind to magic. Consequently, we have become not only skeptical, but disenchanted, insulated, and desensitized. Electronics do all the imagining we think we need. In contrast, primitives and children inhabit a world super-alive with powerful presences that are invisible, like our atoms, molecules, and quarks, but unlike them, personal—caring or malevolent. Sophisticates now—including all your young—sniff at the gullibility of G. K. Chesterton's *Ethics of Elfland*, which shows human decency being as embedded in the natural order of things as gravity and radioactivity.

The poet William Blake demonstrated the kind of mind we have to retain in the face of our admirable accumulation of knowledge and sophistication. It is not a skill very much, if at all, cultivated, even in Catholic schools: "To see a World in a Grain of Sand...And a Heaven in a Wild Flower...Eternity in an hour." What starts getting lost around second grade?

I've never met a single student who expressed the slightest hesitation in accepting science's undisputed claim that the entire horrendously huge universe was once packed into what they call a Singularity, smaller than a period on this page—effect to cause. In the previous chapter, we saw how that same kind of confluence of hints point to the high probability of a Mind-Behind-It-All—effect to cause. However, science delights in playing "What if?" What if we fooled around with this bread mold or these silicon chips?

What if, when this restless Singularity was starting to grow unstable, the Mind-Behind-It-All infused himself into the mix? What if, right there inside that compact "Everything," he "incarnated" himself for the first time—all his intelligence, plans, and purposes? When it exploded in the Big Bang, the presence of God exploded too! Just as, Christians say, happened when the Son entered an ovum and began to grow as a physical human. If that were true, then God is just as real as the energy of atoms, gluons, quarks, and pulsing in all the empty space between them!

Try to imagine all the invisible entities in the room with you right now: gravity, gamma rays, light waves, radio waves, TV signals, ultraviolet rays—and God. Surprise!

Blest are the children whose parents haven't allowed their kids' exclusively rational, left-brain schooling to smother their openness to the magical in life; who took them on nature walks and taught them to listen to the voices in the thunder and songs in the breezes; who taught them to stay friends with God and Jesus and Our Lady; who read the fairy tales to them, who still resonate with Harry Potter and Frodo Baggins and Dorothy Gale; who live in places where neon doesn't cancel out the real stars, and who believe that integrity is more precious than the GDP.

In his book, *Saga: Best New Writings on Mythology*, Jonathan Young writes,

> Mythology allows us to reconnect with a dimension beyond ordinary time. In this moment in history, consumer values dominate the media. Ancient stories give us a chance to visit with eternal characters involved in primal adventures. This can provide perspectives that go beyond trendy concerns with possessions or appearance.*

GOD'S PERSONALITY: LIKES AND DISLIKES

Watch together on the Internet the PBS *Nova* film, *The Miracle of Life* (1980, 58 minutes). It is possible that your child's science teacher has shown it, but it's quite likely that the teacher didn't ask, "What can we conclude about God from that film?" How caring is God? How meticulous, almost like an attentive mother, right? God keeps pushing things to be better. That's what evolution means. You can see that God doesn't like things

---

*Jonathan Young, ed., *Saga: Best New Writings on Mythology* (Ashland, OR: White Cloud Press, 1996), introduction.

to get static, stale, or too comfortable. What does that suggest about the unwelcome "intrusions" in our lives, like adolescence, for one, or setbacks that make you want to quit the race? God is like coaches, teachers, and parents—and vice versa.

God is "into" order and surprise: no shape in nature is perfect, not even the spherical Earth. Everywhere God is "into" death and resurrection—and we haven't yet dipped into Christianity! He's into the balance of yin/yang and very seldom either/or, but almost always more/less—good/evil, masculine/feminine, body/spirit, justice/mercy, immanent/transcendent—neither polarity dominating, each yielding and holding firm. This is a "side" of God that no catechism finds a place for.

God's desire—what people so trippingly describe as "the Will of God"—is written indelibly into the ways everything is made; how it reveals itself. Recall the rock, the apple, the stuffed bear, and the man. Furthermore, the powers of the mind reveal God's purposes in inventing us: continually to quest for wider horizons. Merely to survive is an insult to our Creator. Furthermore, no matter how long or how thoroughly we try to satisfy that hunger with the things we find in this life, it's not enough. That's been true since there have been people.

FOR REFLECTION

What norm can one use to discern a genuine encounter with God from primitive superstition, which makes God a micromanager, scurrying from one human problem to another, pulling off miracles each time. For instance, students will often write of God becoming immanent, "touching" them, when they were in a close-call accident: "I remember suddenly feeling I was safe, that God was with me." Or, just as common, "I knew when we were praying by my grandma's hospital bed that she was going to get better."

First, who's to say that what young people feel on retreats *is* God or "just" the exhilaration that comes from letting down their defenses and allowing themselves to just humanly love and be loved? And who's to say a "merely" human opening is *not* opening to God?

Second, "by their fruits you shall know them." Does an overtly sexual teenage relationship make each a better person outside the relationship—more open, generous, forgiving, and accessible? Or does the relationship make each person more thin skinned, secretive, and snappish? The same is true in "assessing" the presence of God in a person's experience. Does that sense of the presence of God last? Does it spill over into the rest of his or her life? Does it change the person or was it merely like having someone say hello to you in an elevator?

The best choice is to let it be. It could be that critical analysis would be exactly the kind of disenchanting skepticism that turned "Christendom" into "The Economy."

18

THE GOD OF OTHER RELIGIONS

Let me just say that one of the things we need to establish is that God is not a Christian.
—Bishop Desmond Tutu

The most arrogant thing we can do is impose human limits on God—"allowing" God to exist, but only within the parameters that our human minds can encompass. Yet theologians, atheists, and even folks in pubs have been doing it since before there were clocks. God invites endless exploration but never conquest. Reportedly, when Albert Einstein, the Oedipus of the twentieth century, said, "God doesn't play dice with the universe," his colleague, Niels Bohr, said, "Albert, don't tell God what he can do."

Never forget, "The tree comes to me." The Mind reveals his/her self to me.

Arguing the superiority of one's own take on God is as childish as sneering, "My dad could beat up your wimpy old man!" So many academic antagonisms are reducible to schoolyard clashes of one-upmanship. In the fourth century, battles were waged over a single iota in the definition of the Son's relation to the Father; a definition that made the difference between their equality and the Son's inferiority. In philosophy, my professors waged tunnel war among the seminarians against colleagues who differed over whether the distinction between "being" and "nature" existed actually, outside the mind, or merely inside the mind. In *Gulliver's Travels*, the Lilliputians were prepared for war about which end of a soft-boiled egg was "proper" to break. Think of the last time you were in a hot argument and, suddenly, you realized the other party was right, but you kept on arguing.

That's why I started with the unspecified Mind-Behind-It-All! If we begin with God, then we can start the forensic search for God's manner of being and personality habits.

It might be helpful for teachers and parents to begin with some questions: Help me understand what you understand by God, having come this far. Is God more "masculine"—demanding, decisive, aloof, or more "feminine"—welcoming, merciful, consoling? Is God most often far away or close at hand? When you spoke about a time God "touched" you, what was the experience like? Was it like an invisible magnet inside your chest, a warm feeling, fearful, or peaceful? To be honest, does God just "sort of come into existence" when you feel a need for God? When you think of God "close by," who does he look like?

If you're serious about this, don't hesitate to tell them what God's like for you! For example, I tell my classes that I can't really deal meaningfully anymore with the "Everywhere" God. My image of God in prayer is Jesus, a shepherd, but not the wimpy-eyed Jesus of the holy cards. He's a big genial guy, like Hugh Jackman—real shepherds have to haul 150-pound sheep up by their front legs and hold them there for the whole shearing—and he really smells of sheep. The two of us are bumping along in the cab of his pickup, not saying much. What I tell him, he already knows, but he doesn't mind listening. He's my brother and my friend. The important part is that I'm not alone, and I enjoy being with him. The tough part is accepting that he enjoys being with me!

If you find the multiplicity of world religions befuddling, and you don't mind a bit of inelegant language, Google "A Short Guide to Comparative Religions," which is a monument to clarity. But if you want to see how insights into God's will coincide from just about every diverse angle, Google "The Golden Rule in World Religions."

To get an even more startling relief from the usual chill "Rationalized God" of the *Catechism*, you might enjoy reading *The Shack* by William P. Young, which, except for purists, has a refreshing, down-to-earth take on the Trinity. The Father is a big black lady who's cooking all the time and calls you "Honey." The Son is a big carpenter with undeniably Semitic features and who's easygoing, dependable, and Lincolnesque. The Spirit is this Haight-Ashbury chick who scatters light and colors wherever she walks. It beats anything I ever read in Aquinas!

When marshalling *arguments* about God, I recall my own warnings that no one was ever converted by a rational argument, only by a deepening *personal* relationship, like the fellowship Native Americans have with anything natural. At the other extreme, when I get too palsy with God and forget his staggering Otherness, it helps me to get hints from the transcendent folks who stress, validly, if too strongly for me, that God got here first, and made up the rules, and feels no need to change them at my request.

EASTERN RELIGIONS

For those born before the Flower Crusade of the 1950s, the paradoxes of the ethereal Eastern religions pose some roadblocks to insight: the yin and yang of Confucianism, the merging of emptiness and fullness, darkness and light, and existence and nothingness.

Yet that conjunction of apparent antagonisms in the Tao—even the supposed incompatibles of Spirit and Flesh so emphasized by St. Paul—can fuse into one for anyone who allows God the freedom to baffle us. The most basic Christianity is just as replete with apparent contradictions, assertions few of us find puzzling anymore because we've heard them so often: "If you want the first place, take the last place"; "To find yourself, lose yourself"; and "Only in death do we find new life." We ourselves no longer see the absurdity of a triumphant crucifixion.

Mystics like Teresa of Ávila and John of the Cross spoke of the Dark Night of the Soul—the hell that is the only place we truly meet God's light—and they describe union with Christ in sexual images so ripe many worthy Christians would take issue with them. The Anglican John Donne used the same intensely intimate imagery in his Sonnet on the Trinity:

Batter my heart three-person'd God,
...for I,
Except you enthrall [enslave] me, never shall be free,
Nor ever chaste, except you ravish [rape] me.

The analogies may unnerve some, but they can enlighten the insightful.

JUDAISM

The non-Christian religion that most Catholics would claim to know best is Judaism, although their untrue picture of Yahweh was probably assembled more from bad movies than from honest research. My sense is that most Catholic adults imagine the Old Testament's Yahweh to be grumpy, judgmental, irascible, and vengeful. If that image were true, how do we explain Yahweh's indefatigable faithfulness, despite Israel's stupidities and self-centeredness—the exact same qualities Jesus had to face when he finally came himself?

If you have any Jewish friends, ask one of them the elephant question, "What does God look like from where you are?" I guarantee that the response will not be that God is an old grump.

The Jews fused the contraries of Transcendent and Immanent. God is so unutterably "Other" that his presence on Earth sets bushes on fire and is so alive that to look at him would have blinded Moses. Merely touching the Ark containing the Ten Commandments brought death. Even to speak the name of God—"I AM"—was blasphemy, which is precisely what sealed Jesus' death.

However, the Yahweh of the Hebrew Scriptures is also very much immanent. God walks with Adam and Eve companionably in the first garden; he squats by Abraham's tent and allows him to weasel him down about Sodom and Gomorrah, and he tolerates Moses' dithering. More revealing are the friends with whom he chose to hang around: the inconstant, undependable Hebrews. Furthermore, check out the losers he kept picking for heroic tasks. After the failure of Eden, would anyone think of starting over with the same saps who messed up the first experiment? If you're seeking the grandparents of the Hebrew nation, of all the couples on Earth at the time, would you even consider Abram and Sarai—in their nineties and barren as a pair of bricks? For the hero to stand up to Pharaoh, you would choose someone like Charlton Heston, the way Cecil B. DeMille did for *The Ten Commandments*, not the bewildered wimp you find in the actual (inspired) book. In choosing a champion to bring down the nine-foot-six-inch Goliath, which of Jesse's eight sons would you pick: the seven eldest, each of whom was built like Arnold Schwarzenegger, or David, the runt with the slingshot?

You'll find that personality trait consistent in the Christian Scriptures: Mary, a hillbilly girl for the mother of the Messiah, twelve bumbling misfits for the first bishops, including a couple of admitted terrorists and an enemy collaborator, and for the first pope, the guy who apostatized—denied Christ with curses—within a couple hours of his ordination and first Mass, and not to a soldier with a knife at his throat, but to a waitress!

God seems to love to bring the new kid from the back of the chorus to take over temporarily for the lead. Almost every hero/heroine story in our Scriptures is a Cinderella story. So be cautious when you say—or even think—"Oh, I'm nobody." God's on the prowl for you nobodies!

FOR REFLECTION

Some people see God in their consistent, everyday lives as judgmental, demanding, needing to be appeased for our shortcomings. Others see God as cherishing, protective, forgiving even when we feel no need to apologize. Still others (to be honest) find God pretty much irrelevant to their ordinary days, turning to God only when they are in need.

As honestly as you can, describe how you deal with God on a week-to-week, year-to-year basis.

19

THE GOD OF JESUS CHRIST

Let us not come with any patronizing nonsense about
his being a great human teacher. He has not left that
open to us. He did not intend to.

—C. S. Lewis

The real Jesus is not the grammar school Jesus we were first introduced to—and perhaps have yet to outgrow. The genuine Jesus wasn't the Warm Fuzzy of our cowboy hymns or treacly holy cards, posed for by innocent novice nuns. Yet how many Catholic adults have discovered a more appealing Jesus who might have a chance with our students and children? Such a "wuss" simply could *not* have attracted the twelve hard-handed and hard-nosed men, much less the huge crowds he apparently drew. What magnetized them was that he was utterly unlike the usual pale, sheltered rabbi. He was shockingly down-to-earth, intimidatingly *honest*. His enemies accused him of being a glutton and a drunkard; he chummed around with the dregs of his society—lepers and prostitutes, the ritually unclean.

Jesus was an *outlaw*. He rode roughshod over inhuman religious rules. He publicly called the hierarchy of his religion "showoffs...poseurs...hypocrites...corrupters...blind fools...whitewashed tombs...tangle of snakes...prophet killers, etc."

Why couldn't Jesus have postponed so many miracles till the day *after* the Sabbath? What was he trying to *prove*? He was *asking* for it; *daring* them! That's not the standard-issue image that most of us, and our children, have been routinely offered of the model Christian.

If Jesus were simply "mannerly," like the Jesus many Catholics still imagine, and like the Jesus in all the movies, why in heaven's name would they have wanted to *execute* him?

The most practical reason to eliminate him was that he was too dynamic to keep around, a charismatic nonconformist who was attracting too much attention. Additionally, he was pointing out very real flaws in an establishment that ruled more by fear than by persuasion, an elite whose only support for a very comfortable lifestyle was the very Temple he threatened to supplant. "You don't understand," the high priest told his apprehensive colleagues. "It's better that one man die than that we lose the whole nation" (John 11:50).

However, that wasn't the "realest" motive: "For this reason the Jews were seeking all the more to kill him, because he was not only breaking the sabbath, but was also calling God his own Father, thereby making himself equal to God" (John 5:18). At his trial, the high priest put him under *oath*: "Are you the Messiah, the Son of the Blessed One?" And Jesus answered back, right in his face, "I am" (Mark 14:61–62). Take it or leave it. Either he was, truly, who he claimed to be, or he was a con man, or a madman. There is no other alternative. Judge those alternatives against the background of everything else Jesus said and did, and decide where you stand.

I've come to believe that one of *the* most fearsome aspects of adolescence, at least from puberty to marriage, is the seismic shift required to go from someone endlessly provided for to being oneself a provider. The shift is as contrary as the passive and active voice of verbs that are a nifty little test of whether the shift has even begun. Has a child moved from "It got broken" to "I broke it"? Like so many other preconditions for Christianity, until a youngster has at least gotten that far, feeling responsible, the best any teacher or parent can hope for are the residual animal motivations of fear and hope of reward. They can't yet *comprehend* acting on principle.

You can see the shift in the radical difference between the "Thou shalt not's" of the Hebrew commandments, and the weasel-proof positive admonitions of Jesus' only two commandments: "Love God by loving the neighbor." There are no loopholes there. Genuine love simply does not ask, "How far can I go before...?"

Furthermore, check out the only question Jesus puts forward to judge whether your one life was worth God's investment in you. At the Last Judgment (Matt 25), there is only *one* question. On the one hand, it's *not* any of the World's questions: How much did you make? How much of the Monopoly board did you own, or how often was your name in the papers? Nor will it be: How often were you married? How often did you miss Mass, or did you disobey any Church law or doctrine?

There is only one question: "I was hungry...I was thirsty...I was naked. I was the one they called 'loser,' 'slut,' 'wetback,' 'queer.' How did you deal with me?"

Recall the three questions about the book's opening question: "What does 'Success' mean to you as an individual?" (1) Making it, (2) Being un-Bad, (3) Kindness, or (4) All of the above. I suspect most parents and their children really, really want (4). Good luck. None is automatic.

How can you achieve the first place by taking the last place? Remember that there are *two* races heading in opposite directions: the James Bond Race and the Mother Teresa Race. The core question is not how far you succeed in which direction; the question is in which direction is your heart sincerely heading?

Just as we are "made" human by reason of our parentage, we're "made" Christian by baptism. However, each of those "conferrals" is not of a fully functional reality. Each is a *potential* that has to be *freely* activated. Humanity is a spectrum that does include (marginally) pimps and pushers at the low end just above other animals, through increasingly more evolved individuals to such worthies as Lincoln and Mandela. Christianity includes, *pro forma*, anyone whose name is in a parish registry, people who write a Christian denomination when checking into a hospital or the military, people who truly see Christ in their suffering neighbors, through cloistered nuns and jungle doctors, and the whole host of us trying our best, to the whole intimidating Communion of Saints, whose full-hearted self-giving strikes us into awe.

Opening one's Christian potential doesn't "pop on" automatically with the number of years in Christian religious education, no matter how much it cost. Nor does it click on in confirmation, nor, for that matter, even in Holy Orders. Just as the sacrament of Marriage doesn't guarantee a permanent union, much less a blissful one, baptism and all the other sacraments are gifts that require assembly, maintenance, and continual awareness, just like owning a car.

The human soul needs periodic checkups: examining the integrity of the parts and operations; ensuring a clear view before and behind and each side; and checking the shock absorbers, the steering control, and especially the engine that keeps it alive—the soul. The Christian soul needs the same, always checking the vehicle against the owner's manual of the gospels—or the vehicle becomes a rolling wreck.

Like any kind of loving, being Christian *costs*. If not, you may be misusing the words. The reflection question is possibly the Final Judgment: What difference should being a Christian make in your everyday life, in making choices—for instance, choosing a career, investing money, using free time?

It surely ought to be as significant as one's citizenship.

FOR REFLECTION

I ask students what would make a good Christian parent different from a decent, honorable atheist parent. Their invariable response is either "I don't understand the question" or "No difference." This after twelve years of what they call "Catholic brainwashing." In essence, their responses indicate that, to them, being Christian makes no real difference.

What difference should being a Christian make in your everyday choices—for instance, for your children or students, spending money, using your free time?